# NORFOLK

*A People's History*

*This 1856 engraving shows the city and harbor of Norfolk.*

# NORFOLK
## *A People's History*

RUTH A. ROSE

ARCADIA
PUBLISHING

Copyright © 2007 by Ruth A. Rose
ISBN 978-0-7385-2474-0

Published by Arcadia Publishing,
Charleston SC, Chicago IL, Portsmouth NH, San Francisco CA

Printed in the United States

Library of Congress control number: 2007923215

For all general information contact Arcadia Publishing at:
Telephone 843-853-2070
Fax 843-853-0044
E-Mail sales@arcadiapublishing.com
For customer service and orders:
Toll-Free 1-888-313-2665

Visit us on the Internet at www.arcadiapublishing.com

# CONTENTS

Acknowledgments     vii

Introduction     xi

1. The Arrival, the Encounter, and the Overcoming     17

2. The Settlement as Colony: 1724–1790     25

3. We the People: 1790–1860     33

4. The War Between the States and its Aftermath: 1860–1910     42

5. The Customs of a Modern City: 1910–2006     90

6. The Peopling of a Modern City: 1910–2006     104

7. The Challenges of a Modern City: 1910–2006     115

# ACKNOWLEDGMENTS

No matter how small, each individual action is the result of the wisdom and efforts of many people. It is appropriate, then, to acknowledge and thank each one of them here for the time they shared, the information they provided, the technical assistance they offered, and their overall support for this project.

In the early stages when the idea for this book was not clearly formed, it was Wiley Francisco and Tom Jones who offered the endless hours of listening and critiquing that were necessary to establish the foundational thesis upon which the book would rest. During this time it was also Terri L. Bishirjian and Mary and Michael Loumeau who listened and provided encouragement. As it became clear that this book on Norfolk would require endless hours of interviews and the sharing of personal and family stories, documents, and photographic materials, it was Bernadine White, Nick and Mary Vorlas, Frances Murray, Dr. Mildred Jordan, Connie Coppage, Cheryl and Clarence Bunch, Demetra Protogyrou, Joe Chan, Dr. Alan and Edwina Bergano, Gary Ma, Tim Liu, Sister Grace Malonzo, and Clayton and Mildred Francisco who all so generously helped to give texture and personal dimension to the Norfolk story.

It would be foolhardy to try to write a historical overview of Norfolk without consulting the very wise and knowledgeable City Historian Peggy Hale McPhillips. Without her willingness to be of assistance and her thoughtful and kind advice, the project might have steered into troubled waters or not gotten done at all. Certainly, Troy Valos and Robert B. Hitchings, librarians of the Sargent Memorial Room at the Kirn Memorial Library went well beyond the call of duty in assisting me in this project. They were certainly invaluable in helping to compile the photographs for the book as well as offering insight into resources and information for the completion of the project. The majority of the photographs in this book are from the photograph files in the Sargent Memorial Room of the Kirn Memorial Library. The photographs, which have been reprinted from private sources, are appropriately noted in the text.

A very special thanks goes to Susan Bernard for her thoughtfulness in making connections for this project. I am especially appreciative of her having introduced me to Edward Beard, who provided a great deal of insight into the Norfolk story and its development. I am grateful to him for providing me with an overview of the city and for allowing me to publish his perspective on the history and development of Norfolk and also for his view on the ways that Norfolk can move along in the 21st century.

Certainly not to be forgotten in this acknowledgement is my indebtedness to all those who listened, read drafts, and provided encouragement in the 11th hour. Both Tom Barney and Michael Teller were extremely generous in providing me with a reader's reaction to the manuscript. In addition, they both supplied personal information that greatly enhanced my understanding of aspects of the social dynamics of immigration. I also wish to thank Peter Wallenstein, who shared his considerable knowledge of the process of getting words from idea to page.

Even though this book relied primarily upon "observing participant fieldwork," one of the mainstays of anthropological technique, along with oral histories and individual interviews, I would be remiss if I did not provide the reader with a list of excellent sources on the history of Norfolk referenced here. They are: James D. Anderson, *The Education of Blacks in the South 1860–1935*; Tommy Bogger, *Free Blacks in Norfolk, Virginia, 1790–1860*; Dick Nolan, *Benjamin Franklin Butler*; Thomas C. Parramore, Peter C. Stewart, and Tommy L. Bogger, *Norfolk: The First Four Centuries*; Helen C. Roundtree, *Pocahontas, Powhatan, Opechancanough*; Marvin W. Schlegel, *Conscripted City*; George H. Tucker, *Norfolk Highlights 1584–1881*; Thomas J. Wertenbaker and Marvin W. Schlegel, *Norfolk: Historic Southern Port*; and Forrest R. White, *Pride and Prejudice: School Desegregation and Urban Renewal in Norfolk*. These books are excellent sources for serious history enthusiasts who wish to discover in greater detail the facts of Norfolk's development from an English colony to a city "to come home to now."

And of course I am most appreciative of Candace Rose's willingness to provide the necessary quiet time, to consent to editing the almost final drafts, and to sacrifice a vacation in order to make it possible for me to complete this project. The Ronald Thompson family's support of and encouragement for this project has been immeasurable as well.

Most of all, I wish to express my heartfelt appreciation by saying a very special thank you to my editor at Arcadia Publishing, Jim Kempert. Jim demonstrated an unwavering belief in this book during all of its phases. He was able to provide the necessary balance between being a no-nonsense stickler for deadlines and details as well as being a sympathetic encourager. Jim did not give up even in those frustrating moments when I became disillusioned about this project ever getting written. He did not waver and always found a way to provide a solution that would motivate me to completion. Jim is the kind of editor every writer dreams of having!

# INTRODUCTION

When this project was first conceived, it was my intention to document the historical contributions of the many different ethnic groups who have made and continue to make up this city and who are responsible for what the city is today. Further, I intended to uncover why there is so little evidence of these contributions in the common culture of Norfolk and also why there appears to be no real Norfolk culture: no Norfolk speech, no Norfolk words, no Norfolk customs, no Norfolk foods, no Norfolk dress, no Norfolk anything.

After months and months of research on the public record and hours of interviews with members of various ethnic groups and many private hours of reflection, the reason why Norfolk in spite of its multi-cultural, multi-ethnic heritage, its connection to the sea, and its dependence on international trade, remains to this day a "generic" American city, has eluded me. Clearly, Norfolk is a city that has had and still has all the components of a dynamic heterogeneous blending of cultures. When we think of cities where this interaction has taken place, New York, New Orleans, and San Francisco immediately come to mind. They are only a few of the more famous, interesting, and cosmopolitan places in our nation where the city has developed a common culture from the various immigrant groups that have inhabited their boundaries. This blending is not a "puree" where, for example, different vegetables are blended together until the individual parts are not distinguishable and a new taste is formed. It is rather a "ratatouille" where each vegetable is lightly sauteed separately, then added together to be cooked in a common skillet allowing the individual flavors to combine while retaining their unique shapes and characteristics. This was the story I wished to tell. But the story that revealed itself to me did not subscribe to my formula. It is a story I believe worth telling, although there have been moments when I have had my doubts.

*Norfolk: A People's History* was to be a part of the Making of America series from Arcadia Publishing. The series focused on the contributions to local history of cities across the nation, highlighting the uniqueness and development of individual communities—the *e pluribus unum*—in the making of our nation. In spite of this author's best efforts to conform to the structure required for the series, neither the ethno-historical research nor the fieldwork results nor the oral histories lent themselves to that format. Because this book on Norfolk's people's history was, we believed, an important addition to the Arcadia catalogue, it was decided to abandon its inclusion in the series and allow the content to determine the shape of the text.

This book on Norfolk is, most certainly, an important addition. The subtitle, "A People's History," refers not to specific individuals but instead to the various groups or peoples who make up the history, character, and personality of the city—the cultural history. What indeed is a cultural history and how does it differ from history as we are used to thinking of it? For the most part, when we think of the history of a region or city we think of the major events such as battles, natural disasters, geographical factors, economic structure, and individuals who have contributed to the making of the city as we know it. What we seldom consider are the groups of people who comprise the population—the way they live, celebrate life, form social partnerships, establish economic class structures, and create religious affiliations.

When thinking of Norfolk, people come to mind, normal American citizens, ordinary everyday working people. People who make the moments of their lives into an opera filled with drama, excitement, ceremonies, rites of passage, love lost, love gained, births, deaths, dreams fulfilled and dreams lost on their way to daily living. Lives filled with what one could call a people's opera and what anthropologists are fond of calling "culture."

Of course, the focus on culture as the primary driving force is predicated upon the belief that cities are organic, that they are created by and for people. Cities take their shape and form their contours based upon the needs of the people who establish them and not the other way around. In most people's minds, Norfolk is frequently associated with the armed services, the Navy in particular. Ask most men who were stationed here during the wars about Norfolk's culture and they will fondly reminisce about endless hours of "sin and skin" on Granby and Main Streets. Norfolk, aside from housing the largest amphibious naval base in the United States, also provided if not the largest, then one of the most intense, pleasure centers for rest and relaxation leave in the area.

But underneath this free-wheeling laissez-faire culture that sailors saw, Norfolk was a serious city intent on maritime commerce and trade. A city of multiple ethnicities and fundamental capitalism all focused upon the relationship between capital, production, and profit. Norfolk from early times was the city of opportunity and the city of hope—the port of possibility. Many people came to improve their economic circumstances and many others used Norfolk as a stop on their way to larger northern cities.

For years Norfolk has been losing a sizable portion of its population to the surrounding suburban areas in Hampton Roads. So at the beginning of the 21st century, the City of Norfolk initiated a "Come Home To Norfolk Now" campaign. This title seemed an odd choice of words for a city largely imprinted on most people's minds as a "Southern Sin City," a Navy town, a smallish and rather shabby port city. Notwithstanding those impressions, the campaign is designed specifically to reinvent Norfolk as a progressive upper south city of young urban professionals, empty nesters, second career retirees, and all who wish to trade in their white picket fence lives in the suburbs for modern city living. It is designed to provide the amenities of upscale urban living for the person who wants to be close to restaurants, museums, shopping, and night life, and be in the forefront of Norfolk's community renaissance. Many of the older, more conventional neighborhoods are being redeveloped with an eye toward providing larger housing stock that can satisfy the special requirements of modern families in higher income brackets. Increasing the tax base is a major objective in many older cities and Norfolk is no exception. This people's history of Norfolk attempts to present a broad historical overview of the peopling of the city for the newcomer as well as the native. The intent of this holistic presentation is to provide some insight into what makes the culture and city of Norfolk a place to come home to now.

Our story begins in chapter one in 17th century Europe, during its age of globalization. This view reveals the motivation for the English drive for overseas colonial expansion. It sets the context for the settlement at Jamestown, but not in the usual way. It begins with the people whom the settlers encountered there, the indigenous peoples. Because of the dearth of written material and oral tradition, the primary source material is Helen C. Rountree's ethno-historical *The Powhatan of Virginia*. Her ethnography culls together written documents, 20th-century interviews, archeological material, and first hand accounts of indigenous life in this region.

In chapter two, the settlement becomes a crown colony. Norfolk is made into a town, develops into a borough, and participates in the Revolutionary War. Some of the seeds of its character are developed during this period when the British set the colony's shape and structure with the aid of the Scots from Northern Ireland. In chapter three freedom arrives, Norfolk becomes a part of the nation, and religious freedom is established. Along with the right to worship comes the right to establish churches other than the Church of England or Anglican Church. This is a major shift that sets the pace for the ideology of religious tolerance. It is during this period that we begin to recognize one of the major ethnic groups that contributes to the cultural dynamics of the city.

Chapter four covers Norfolk during the Civil War years. These were the years that helped to shape our destiny as a nation and Norfolk as a city. With the end of the war came major shifts in economic and educational possibilities and a new period of cultural diversity. Chapter five brings us into the 20th century when the ideas, customs, and habits that shaped Norfolk's culture are recounted. Beginning with chapter six the peopling of modern Norfolk is considered. Important to the discussion are the population shifts due to the waves of immigrants arriving in its port. In chapter seven, the challenges brought on by growth and by being a part of the modern world are examined. We see the interaction of the citizens and the city in the process of accommodation. This chapter brings us to a time when Norfolk begins to hit its stride and work through some of the conflicting issues of this period. Norfolk is challenged with forming its own voice in response to much larger issues not just as a Virginian city but as an American city, and with what it is and what it stands for. The results of these struggles help Norfolk to define itself in the 21st century.

Unlike a conventional history book developed in a linear sequence, this one does not progress chronologically through the decades from the arrival at Jamestown to the present. What appears as each chapter opens is often a central moment in time in a particular period with snapshots of discussion moving back and forth between decades from a central midpoint. The points of discussion in this little book center around a particular concept, an ideological moment, or a central event in order to focus the reader's attention on the daily issues that concern real people who inhabit cities.

As with all books, this one has an intended audience. Of course it is my hope that everyone will read this book and enjoy it; nevertheless, I did envision a certain reader as I told the story of the city's development and growth. I imagined speaking to a person who had come to Norfolk for the first time in recent years, and was quite taken with its progress. They might be here for a convention, taking a cruise, doing business, or just visiting relatives, and they would want to know how Norfolk came to be such a charming city—so modern and yet so approachable. The other group of readers who formed my intended audience were Norfolk's citizens: those who have lived their entire lives here, never giving much thought to the overall composition of the city or its patterns of daily life. For them I wanted to tell a story in which they, along with their fellow citizens, would be celebrated, as well as a story in which they could see themselves reflected anew and as a part of a wonderful, heterogeneous whole. Certainly the serious students of history were an intended part of the audience too, even though for them the older, more traditional books on Norfolk's history might be more satisfying.

So then, as readers move back and forth through the centuries, they have an opportunity to view Norfolk from the perspective of those whose daily lives helped to give it shape, tone, and texture as it moved along the evolutionary path from agrarian to industrial. This little text is primarily the story of the citizens and visitors who have made Norfolk what it is today. Of course the stories of great men and famous events are told here as well, but only as a backdrop to the lives and culture of the people who make up this wonderful city that we are all invited to come home to now.

# 1. THE ARRIVAL, THE ENCOUNTER, AND THE OVERCOMING

The story of "coming to America" has been told so many times and in so many ways that by now the versions have distilled into a romanticized tale of the pursuit of religious freedom by a group of oppressed ascetic Protestants. This version, ever popular in legions of elementary school textbooks, obscures the primary intent of the voyages by shifting the focus from an economic pursuit, which was the initial and chief intention, to a religious one. Taking a moment to look back, we can get a glimpse of the atmosphere and the imperatives of 17th century England. In doing so a broader picture emerges that provides a context and perhaps even a better understanding of what the real colonial endeavor was all about.

Our story begins in the Old World during its period of expansion. England was not as commercially nor militarily strong as either Spain or Portugal. During this period, it was plagued by a declining feudal system with displaced peasants who were becoming a burden on the economy. The nascent merchant and artisan classes were increasingly in need of wider markets for the distribution of their goods. These factors along with others made the possibility of New World settlements an attractive prospect. A colonial market would allow for a wider distribution of English goods and for the import of commodities from the New World. This made for a very enticing economic prospect.

The 17th century was also a time when both curiosity and greed were abundant. Europe's curiosity had been sparked by the earlier travel accounts of the Portuguese encounters with strange peoples who had even stranger customs and the new varieties of spices and products from the East brought back by the explorers. This curiosity was further fueled by Spanish accounts of their arrival or, as it has been so often described in most school textbooks, their "discovery" of the New World, which contained an abundance of important goods and natural resources. The successful navigation around the Cape of Good Hope to India also contributed to heightened interest in territories beyond Europe's shores. Other parts of the globe were increasingly viewed as potential sites for acquiring supplies and resources that would enable Europe to fuel its economies. Dazzled by the variety and wealth of commodities brought back by the explorers, European crowns were desirous of their shares of the pie. This was particularly true for 17th century England. It had become used to the imported goods acquired from the expeditions of the Spanish and Portuguese. The desire to have a stake in overseas trade for itself led Great Britain to seek its own steady source of resources for consumption and for embellishing the economy.

In the quest to seek worlds beyond its shores, England was late to enter the game of overseas expansion. As early as the late 1500s, an attempt had been made at colonizing the New World by Sir Humphrey Gilbert. Sir Gilbert was not successful on his first try in 1579. The breakup of his fleet made it necessary for him to return to England. On his second try, in 1583, he was able to reach what is now St. John's Bay, Newfoundland, and establish it as a foothold in the New World for the queen. Unfortunately for him, his return voyage was marred by the loss of his crew. The following year, Sir Gilbert's brother Sir Walter Raleigh was given his brother's charter by Queen Elizabeth. After sending out a small group to survey territory farther down the coast, Sir Walter Raleigh engaged a group of settlers commanded by Sir Richard Grenville. This group of settlers returned to England a year later with memories of such severe and harsh conditions that they would not return. Nevertheless, as the story goes, Raleigh would not be deterred by these failures. He dispatched three ships with a total of approximately 115 people of all ages and genders to the area we now refer to as Roanoke Island in 1587 under the leadership of John White. After some time White returned to England to bring back desperately needed supplies for the settlement. Neither luck nor fate was on White's side; when he returned to Roanoke Island with the supplies, he found little remaining evidence of the settlers. To this day the mystery of what became of them remains. Were they the victims of hostile indigenous peoples or had they starved to death or had there been an epidemic that killed them all off?

When King James I of England granted a charter to the Virginia Company of London on April 10, 1606, it was for the purpose of establishing a profitable colonial settlement in the New World. The king specified that all colonists must be English and that the Church of England be the official church of the colony. As was the custom in those days, the London Company was set up as a chartered monopoly corporation, a joint stock venture between noblemen, adventurers, and investors and the crown. There were primarily two types of stock offered by the corporation, adventurer shares and planter shares. Adventurer shares appealed primarily to those who were interested in an investment and not the idea of travel. On the other hand, the planter shares had appeal for those whose sense of adventure was greater than their pocketbooks. They could travel to the new colony as a member of the company, establish a settlement, and produce exports for the company. Although planter shares came with a specific time stipulation, three years, they guaranteed profit sharing, food, clothing, and shelter. At the end of the planter's contract he would be entitled to land of his own in the settlement. In order to increase the profitability of these voyages, peasants and religious dissenters were also encouraged to sign on. Most of the time it was peasants who signed on to work for the company in exchange for passage to the new land plus food, clothing, and shelter. Unlike planter shareholders, these indentured servants were not entitled to land of their own at the end of their tenure of seven years, nor were they entitled to a share of the company's profits. In contrast, most of the religious dissenters were able to purchase planter contracts for themselves.

Even though the mission of The Virginia Company was quite clear and opportunities for establishing profitable ventures were available, a great deal of the colonists' time had to be spent on social interaction. The land that the colonists found upon arriving was neither barren nor uninhabited. The terrain, much of which was malaria-infected swampland, contained interlocking waterways, dense vegetation, and variations in climate that made it necessary for the colonists to learn new ways of navigating, taming, and cultivating the land as well as developing medicines to fight off new diseases. In spite of all that, an overwhelming amount of time had to be spent in social intercourse with the indigenous peoples in order to negotiate peace as the colonists continued their expansion deeper into native territories. As the story goes, after some initial hardships the colonists were able to subdue the indigenous inhabitants, master the land, and establish a successful colony. The real story is fraught with tales of fear, hunger, and violence. There are many accounts of confusion, conflict, and outright battles, not all of which end with the colonists as victors.

Nevertheless, the colonists eventually prevailed and were able to survive not only the hostile environment of the New World but also the fluctuations of the Virginia Company's profits, reorganizations, and bankruptcy. In 1624 King James made Virginia a royal colony governed by an appointed governor and an assembly. Not long after, the order was given to establish a "towne." It was believed that by establishing population centers, colonies had a better chance of enduring and stabilizing, which would lead to increased production and more resources and profits for the mother country. Towns also meant families, and families meant stability. So in 1680, King Charles II requested that the royal governor establish towns of 50 acres in all 20 Virginia counties. Norfolk became a town around 1681 when it was laid out by surveyor John Ferebee. It would take another year for the deed to be properly recorded. Historians are not in agreement on whether there were permanent indigenous peoples in this area, but most accept that by the time of the founding of Norfolk, the only people in this region were the Powhatan. The legend goes that originally the Chesipeoc inhabited the region and their principal town was Skicoac. This is in dispute by historians. Some argue that the site that actually became Norfolk was Indian farm land or forest and not inhabited. What seems to be agreed upon is that the first European to own land in what is now Norfolk was Captain Thomas Willoughby, who became a prominent citizen of Norfolk and of Virginia. Although born in England, he is reported to have come to Virginia as a very small boy at around the age of nine on a ship named *Prosperous*. It was a foreshadowing, as it were, of his later success in Norfolk.

Historians of the region give varying accounts of the Chesipeoc presence in the Hampton Roads area. The most popular version is that Wahunsonacock, a Powhatan, had a dream of prophecy of the Powhatan being overtaken by the Iroquois-speaking Chesipeoc who lived to the south. As a result of the dream, the Powhatan destroyed the Chesipeoc, whose main town was Sicoac, said to have been approximately where West Ghent is today. What seems most important in all the varying accounts of the demise of the Chesipeoc is that when their land was settled by the English it was vacant. So in effect it was available to be colonized.

The Powhatan Indians, however, were the strongest and most aggressive group of people with whom the colonists had to contend. They were not "naked savages" as often portrayed in contemporary popular culture. What the Europeans who were invading this new land found was an organized group of people living in harmony with their environment and warring with their neighbors when necessary to settle disputes.

The Powhatan were an Algonquin-speaking people. The Algonquin language family consists of several language groups, but most Algonquin speakers living in close proximity to each other spoke mutually understandable dialects. We can infer many of the features of the Powhatans' language by examining the distinguishing features of the Algonquin language family as a whole. One such interesting feature is the use of affixes. Affixes are the particles or parts of words that are attached to word stems to indicate additional meanings or features of the word. While there are many types of affixes, the most common are prefixes, suffixes, and infixes. Tagalog, spoken in the Philippines, is an example of a language that uses infixes; for example, the stem *bili* adds the infix *-um* and becomes *bumili*, meaning "to buy." English, on the other hand, uses only prefixes and suffixes. A suffix can be added to a verb stem in English to indicate how many are doing the action. For someone learning English this particular feature is often confusing because the suffix "-s" is only added when the subject doing the action is singular. When there are many subjects doing an action, no suffix is added. Other Indo-European languages add suffixes to indicate the number of subjects doing the action. In Spanish, for example, the addition of a suffix to the end of a verb indicates not only how many but also the gender of the subject. In Algonquin languages like Powhatan, a verb can indicate not only the number of persons doing the action and the gender of those persons, but also the direction of the action. Direction markers help to clarify the relationship between the subject, the goal of a particular action, and where the action is coming from or going to. For Algonquin speakers direction is a significant part of communication. For English speakers the more significant part is what was being done by whom, and perhaps how.

A second interesting feature of Algonquin language is the ability of the speaker to indicate inclusiveness or exclusiveness in the first- and second-person plural. In English it is assumed that the use of the pronoun "we" includes the speaker. However, in Algonquin it is possible to indicate the group one is part of and not include oneself in the subject. It is hard for an English speaker to imagine an occasion in which one would need to use "we" and exclude oneself, so it might be easier to understand the benefits of this feature if we look at the second person plural. Often one wishes to say "you" meaning "all of you"—the person spoken to in addition to others in their group. Such cases gave rise to the colloquial terms "you all" or "y'all." But when we do not wish to include the person spoken to in the "you," we employ something like the awkward expression "present company excluded." Algonquin speakers have the option to convey this same meaning in both first- and second-person plural with much more ease and elegance.

These two features of Algonquin languages illustrate the potential difficulty in translating between two language families and the problems the colonists and indigenous peoples must have had in trying to communicate.

Because of the dearth of written material on the subject, anthropologist Helen C. Roundtree's *The Powhatan of Virginia* and *Pocahontas, Powhatan, Opechancanough: Three Lives Changed by Jamestown*, are important sources on the daily lives of the indigenous peoples the English encountered at Jamestown and are summarized and quoted extensively below. Unlike the English whose towns were made up of houses and shops in close proximity to each other with streets laid out on a more or less perpendicular grid, the Powhatan towns were less dense and consisted mostly of small thatched-roof houses. These communities were in almost direct contrast to European towns. The Powhatan lived among nature; that is, their houses and outhouses were not lined up together in rows as they were in England but rather interspersed among trees and gardens. This configuration probably had a great deal to do with the fact that in the Powhatan world view, the land did not belong to the person residing on it; rather, that person had "user rights" to the land and was effectively a tenant. Even though there were paths through the woods that connected towns, the use of streets or roads as a way to transverse territory was not a major feature of their towns. Roundtree points out that the various waterways and canals were instead used as the primary transportation routes. This made it important for not only adults, but also young children, to be able to use a canoe. The rivers and canals did not serve as a boundary between people but as a means of transport to visit relatives, gather reeds for making mats, and get to enemies during war. Because bathing was an essential part of daily life, people used the rivers to bathe as well. The rivers and canals also served as a source of food, providing an effectively endless source of shellfish and other important foods. Shells were also collected from the rivers and used for tools. Roundtree notes:

> The Powhatans were not a farming people. They maintained a combined economy of farming—beans and corn—foraging for plants such as tukahoe. . . . They only raised enough food and raised enough corn for tribute to support their Chief's expenses on diplomatic occasions. They were not accustomed to making the land produce as much as possible of any one thing and then trading for life's other necessities, real or imagined.

They also hunted for deer and wild turkeys; however, they did not, as Roundtree points out, mark firm boundaries on any tract of land. For the Powhatan, "the deer belonged to the hunter who killed it, but the land belonged to everyone who foraged there." The fact that the Powhatan as a group also left their villages two times a year and did not erect any boundaries to mark their territory might also have contributed to the idea of vacant, unclaimed land.

Religion was also an important aspect of the Powhatan way of life. Roundtree notes that because of their environment, there were many hazards and religion was a way of appealing to a higher power for assistance. It also served as a means of dealing with injuries and diseases and the potential for a shortened life span. She also points out that the English assumed that the indigenous peoples would become converts to Christianity and the English culture. To this end, the Anglican Church organized a fund drive throughout England for the express purpose of making a "college" for indigenous children in Henrico. It is important to note that this would not have been a place of post-secondary higher education as we think of colleges today. During that time a college was a school—primarily an elementary school—with perhaps some upper level grades that might be considered secondary. The Powhatan, however, were unreceptive to the idea of a college and resisted any attempts at education. Perhaps they knew or could guess that the enterprise was not for the charitable purpose of expanding their knowledge, but was rather intended to Christianize, civilize, and deculturalize them. This is the first evidence of the attempted use of schooling for social control and cultural transmission, which we will see later was a major factor in the development of education in the United States.

There was little need for the Powhatan to worry because the funds collected each Sunday were never put toward their stated purpose. The Virginia Company continually diverted these donations to pay for other fixed costs such as new supply ships and whatever other expenses they felt were necessary. By 1622 the Powhatan had had enough of the English imposition on their territory and culture and mounted an attack on the settlers. This "Great Assault" as Roundtree calls it, plus mounting debt along with diminishing profits, resulted in the crown taking over the colony in 1624.

# 2. THE SETTLEMENT AS COLONY: 1724–1790

When the crown took over the Virginia territories from the Virginia Company of London in 1624, the area consisted of rural settlements scattered throughout the Tidewater area. The abundance of waterways made it possible for each planter to have his own dock on to which his cargo could be loaded for export to Britain or the West Indies. It also facilitated the import of goods from those places. This system might have gone on endlessly had it not been for an order by King Charles II in 1662 to create a town at James City. Wertenbaker & Schlegel note in *Norfolk: Historic Southern Port*, "the Assembly . . . passed an act, for the erection of a town at 'James City,' where all the tobacco of the three nearest counties was to be brought for storing and export." This attempt to create a town "for which there was no need met with the failure it deserved, and the homes were 'not made habitable' and fell down before they were finished."

Even though this first attempt at centralizing the site of exportation did not succeed, another one did. By 1680, the king declared that unless the assembly created towns in Virginia, he would require ships loading in Virginia to load only at designated places. Therefore, it was decided that each county would establish towns of 50 acres each at the cost of 10,000 pounds of tobacco and cask. Further, each town was to be subdivided into lots of one-half acre each for the purchase price of 100 pounds of tobacco, according to Wertenbaker & Schlegel. By 1681 county surveyor John Ferebee had divided the land into 51 lots and designated the town's Main Street to run from east to west and its north-south axis named the "street that leadeth into the woods." This street is now famously known as Church Street with the part of it closest to the Elizabeth River designated St. Paul's Boulevard in recognition of the borough church. After commanding that trade in the colonies would be contingent upon the establishment of towns, in 1681, King Charles vetoed the act to create a town at James City. Nevertheless, either in defiance or as a result of lack of communication, the town continued with its plans. Growth of "towne Norfolk" got off to a slow start until after 1691, when the county was divided in two to make Lower Norfolk County and Princess Anne County.

Even with the development of towns, the area could still be called rural and rugged. Structurally the town was made up of a collection of warehouses, workshops for shoes, barbering, and smithing, and living spaces of single- or double-storied structures with chimneys at either end. The design was motivated more by practicality and use than by beauty. Warehouses, municipal buildings, offices, marketplaces, and houses were all situated in close proximity to each other. Instead of sidewalks and paved streets, there were dirt paths and roads that were narrow, winding, and unpaved. When it rained one could expect not only to get wet but thoroughly muddy as well. Often one would have to navigate around and through standing water. This was a problem because many of the ditches and puddles contained floating debris of all kinds—market trash, household trash, warehouse trash, and all other sorts of trash. The municipal codes we chafe under today that provide us with standardized levels of hygiene were nonexistent during colonial times. Moreover, no attention appears to have been given to aesthetic considerations. Living spaces were designed to provide shelter rather than representations of one's status in life. In the typical house one entered through a foyer connected to a hall that ran straight through the house from the front to the back. On one side of the hall, usually the left, was the public room—the room that represented the housekeeping style of the residents much as our living rooms or great rooms do today. On the right side was the dining room where Sunday meals and official meals were taken. The end of the hall led into a garden used for a vegetable patch and perhaps a few flowers and shrubs. The kitchen was an independent structure not attached to the house. Food cooked there had to be transported to the dinning room to be served. The kitchen also functioned as a bath house on Saturday nights. Taking turns, each family member bathed in the "tin tub," which was usually placed beside the stove. Excretory functions required another separate structure located away from the house behind the kitchen.

Of course, it is tempting to imagine that the colonial town resembled the modern town fashioned in the model of "new urbanism." However, the mixed use towns of today with their sidewalks, corner potted shrubs, and handicap-cut sidewalks bear no resemblance to the mixed use towns of colonial times. Towns were used initially as central places for commerce. They were places where maritime trade occurred and where local farmers could dispose of their produce either at market or for shipment to other areas. Towne Norfolk was a centralized commercial location where business came first and family life was supported when and where necessary.

In the 150 years between the crown's takeover of the settlement from the Virginia Company in 1624 and the start of the Revolutionary War in 1775, Norfolk grew from a county in 1637, to a towne in 1680, and then a borough in 1737. With each expansion, its physical structure developed, its importance in the region increased, and its population grew. As noted above, Norfolk was a thriving, bustling, dusty little merchant community full of unplanned residences interspersed among the warehouses, workshops, and commercial properties necessary for maritime trade. Houses were often made out of brick, but they were not built to last a lifetime.

The centralizing of import and export to Norfolk's harbor contributed to the town's importance. All freight from the surrounding regions was delivered to Norfolk to be shipped to either the West Indies or to England. This of course precipitated an increase in population if for no other reason than the need for more workers to handle the merchandise. Norfolk's population increased to approximately 1,000 by the time of the Revolution, not including the enslaved population who worked mainly on the docks and as house servants in the city. (The non-urban rural enslaved population is also not included in this count.)

Even with all the excitement that port cities engender, Norfolk's ethnic composition remained somewhat constant. This was not as surprising as it might seem today. As a British colony, it was important for Norfolk to have cultural uniformity. This ensured that British folkways and mores were understood, accepted, and maintained, thereby eliminating the possibility of any kind of ethnic strife or foreign ethnic "pollution," a common fear at the time. While the people's way of life resembled a much more sparse and austere version of English port city life, there was continuous pressure on the colony to produce for the crown, causing people to work tirelessly to meet the demand. Holidays and Sundays provided the only opportunities for some semblance of relaxation or fun, and they were taken full advantage of. There are many accounts of Norfolk's fondness for the theater, for example. George Tucker, in his book *Norfolk Highlights: 1584–1881*, described the beginning of the local theater scene: "Norfolk's recorded theatrical history dates from November 17, 1751, when a company of strolling actors headed by Walter Murray and Thomas Kean presented 'The Recruiting Officer' a comedy by the Irish playwright George Farquhar in 'Captain Newton's Great Room.' "

Cultural uniformity did not mean social class uniformity. Norfolk's population was comprised of people form various segments of the English class structure, from petty criminals to indentured servants to adventurers to merchants. At the top of the pecking order were the clergy and professionals—those with specialized training and the crown's representatives. In the next rank were the merchants and mariners—officers and sea captains. They were followed by tradespeople who were for the most part skilled artisans—barbers, shoemakers, carpenters, bricklayers, tanners, sailmakers, watchmakers, and so on. Artisans were independent, prosperous, and literate. They learned their crafts through the process of apprenticeship, and one requirement of their training was to be taught how to read, write, and do basic arithmetic. The bottom rung of the social class ladder was comprised of the average sailor, the common laborer, and domestic worker. Often they were contract laborers—indentured servants whose service was contracted for a given length of time, after which they could obtain their independence. The Africans who comprised the largest percentage of the workforce were in a separate category defined by race. Within this category there was a parallel structure, with the free African at the top and the unskilled laborer at the bottom.

While it may seem odd from the perspective of today's society where religion is much more of a personal matter, in the world of the 17th century, religion loomed large and pervaded every aspect of a person's life. So it is not hard to see that by limiting formal religious expression to one official church—the Church of England—uniformity of belief, ideas, and lifestyle could be easily maintained.

The Protestant Reformation took on a slightly different form in England. The break with Roman Catholicism did not occur initially over doctrinal issues, but rather as a political break when Henry VIII wished to divorce his heirless wife. In order to do so the king, by an act of parliament in 1534, had himself and his heirs declared the head of the Church in England, which would become known as the Anglican Church. Changes in doctrine developed over time in the reigns of King Edward VI and Queen Elizabeth I. By 1559, during the reign of King Edward VI, an agreement was reached that established the Anglican Creed of 42 articles. This would later be refined by Queen Elizabeth I in 1563 to 39 articles. Although Queen Elizabeth was in favor of a reformed church, she wanted a church that would not take an extreme theological position. The Anglican Creed established a middle ground between Catholicism, Calvinism (a more austere form of Protestantism), and Lutheran Protestantism. Ultimately it would be the differences between the traditionalists and the Puritans, who wanted a more purified church, that would lead to the exodus of the Puritans from England to the New World after 14 years in Holland. Nevertheless, the Anglican Church and its ritual would remain close to the Roman Catholic form.

The first Anglican Church in Lower Norfolk County was established at Sewell's Point on land where the Norfolk Naval Base is located today. Even though there were many believers of other denominations who would arrive in Norfolk, such as the Calvinist Presbyterians, Baptists, and later Methodist Episcopals, the strategy of cultural and religious hegemony diminished the opportunities for social discord and facilitated the colonial project of mercantile commerce.

When Lower Norfolk County was carved out of Elizabeth City County in 1637, the population was made up of English, Scotch-Irish, African, and some indigenous people. We are all familiar to some degree with the colonial life of Africans, indigenous peoples, and the British. However, little has been written about the Scottish immigrants. Perhaps this omission occurs because the Scots are subsumed under the British umbrella and their effect on the development of the colonies is seldom singled out. However, their contributions to the commercial and cultural life of Virginia, and the Tidewater area in particular, have been significant. Although Scots came to the colonies from all parts of Scotland, it was the group often referred to as Scotch-Irish whose legacy has been important in Norfolk and its environs. The name Scotch-Irish refers to the descendents of the Scot migration to Northern Ireland after the Irish Rebellion in 1608. King James I believed that having the Scots occupy Ulster County would keep the Irish at bay. The Scots pushed the Irish further and further back into the countryside, forming the largest contingent in the region. They were culturally and racially Scot and resisted all attempts at assimilation with the Irish. Their allegiance was to the crown in spite of their distrust of the British, to whom they were philosophically and religiously opposed. At the core of this antagonism was a fundamental difference in religious ideology. The Scotch-Irish were Calvinist Presbyterians and abhorred the British insistence on their swearing allegiance to the Church of England. By the time the opportunity to resettle in North America was proposed in the late 17th century, it was seen as a way to lessen the increasing economic restrictions and religious harassments imposed on them by the British. Emigration to North America offered the promise of economic and religious freedom. Little did they realize that they would find British religious strictures in Virginia as well. Nevertheless, Norfolk and the surrounding counties were much more focused upon economic incentives and turned a blind eye to deviant religious practices as long as they were not formalized and did not compete with the official church.

The Scots were Protestant, which was important to the British as it helped to establish a firm barrier against the possibility of a Catholic invasion. (Although it is hard to imagine today, the obsession with the perceived power of the Pope to command absolute authority over his flock was an ever present fear for early Protestants. Nevertheless, vestiges of this fear were still evident as recently as the 1960s when John F. Kennedy ran for president.) As it had done during the years of the Virginia Company, the crown limited immigration to people who were British subjects, by and large. This ethnocentrism was driven in part by the economic and religious currents of the day—mercantilism and religious reformation. Protestantism placed the individual in the center of their responsibility to God, especially with the elimination of confession and the idea that all believers could apprehend God directly. It thereby shifted responsibility for the success of one's life onto the individual believer. This was a very empowering notion and combined with settlement in a new land, it offered the believer the promise of unlimited possibility. Throughout the 18th century government control over trade and industry squelched many visions of fortunes that migrants might have had. Britain's mercantilist philosophy viewed the colonies as outposts for the production of raw materials and gold and silver to support the crown and the home economy. To ensure that the efforts of the colonies would directly benefit the mother country, the Navigation Acts or Acts of Trade were created. These acts required that all ships transporting goods for export and import between the mother country and the colonies must be made in the colony or the mother country and that no goods could be carried on them that were not designated for a British colony or the mother country. This excluded any independent trade between the colony and another nation or colonial country. These acts would eventually be the cause of enough discomfort to be a contributing factor in the American struggle for independence. The Scots immigrated to the new world aware of these limitations and attempted to make their way in spite of them.

The Scots were a hearty people, used to rugged terrain in both Scotland and Ireland, and they possessed a degree of sophistication as a result of their religious beliefs, which enabled them to carve out a niche for themselves in the New World. Even though the English had been here for quite some time and had been successful in establishing a settlement, they were not able to conquer the land. So Norfolk and its environs were still dense with swamp and forest. It was the Scots who were able to do the tracking and overland work of pushing the indigenous people further back into the interior, taking their land for themselves and bargaining for skins, furs, and other goods that could be traded at market. They were also successful as tobacco merchants, dominating the growing, processing, warehousing, and shipping of tobacco to the Old World. Glasgow, Scotland outpaced Bristol to become the center for the import of tobacco in Europe.

In an odd sort of way the Scotch-Irish also dominated education and cultural life. This was possible in part due to their religious convictions about learning and their veneration of classical training. In an agrarian society where the primary focus was on commerce and where no formal schools existed, itinerant Scotch-Irish men were often hired to be tutors for prosperous planter children. The tutor would ride from plantation to plantation providing lessons on the European classics and instruction in Latin and Greek and frequently Hebrew. Along with book learning, students were also given lessons in cultural arts.

With American independence came an opening up of the former British colony to peoples from throughout Europe and even, in one case in Norfolk, to Europeans from the Caribbean. Norfolk officials were confronted with evidence of gross torture and suffering as a result of the 1793 uprising in Haiti and felt compelled to offer aid and assistance when they saw French refugees, many with their Haitian servants, packed onto vessels docked at the port. It was a grim sight that prompted Thomas Newton Jr. of Norfolk to write to the governor requesting aid to assist the refugees. In an unusual move, a $2,000 grant was appropriated by the state of Virginia to be used for assisting the refugees. This was certainly appreciated—Norfolk, bustling though it was, would not have been able to absorb the additional population without assistance. Not all of the French refugees remained in Norfolk, however. Some continued on to Baltimore and beyond, but many stayed and settled here. In *Norfolk Highlights* George Tucker notes, "When the French refugees came from Haiti to Norfolk as a result of the uprising in 1793, the borough became more cosmopolitan." Living in Norfolk today it is hard to even imagine a French presence here. Certainly there are no observable vestiges of the former cosmopolitan life Tucker described.

With freedom of choice and freedom from colonial restrictions, Norfolk was now poised at the beginning of the 19th century to forge its way into the world on its own terms.

# 3. WE THE PEOPLE:
## 1790–1860

A major thrust of Norfolk's population diversity in the early 19th century began in the late 18th century with the arrival in 1790 of boatloads of French from the West Indies escaping revolt in their homeland of Santo Domingo, or as it is known today, Haiti. As noted earlier, the mayor of Norfolk felt compelled to aid the refugees after observing their pitiful condition. After receiving medical attention and getting back on their feet, many of the French moved on to other parts of the region and to points north like Baltimore, Philadelphia, and New York, although a sizeable number of them remained in Norfolk. How odd this juxtaposition must have been between the English or, more precisely the Scots, who were known universally for their austerity, parsimony, and dedication to hard work, and the French who were known for their joie de vivre outlook on life. According to Parramore, Stewart, and Bogger in *Norfolk, the First Four Centuries*:

> The French presence almost certainly contributed to the first stirrings of community conscience in the new Norfolk, to a livelier sense of Enlightenment thought, perhaps to an enhanced aestheticism and sensitivity to manners. And, maybe most of all, the French sojourn provided Norfolk with an opportunity to delve into the wellsprings of its humanity. The community's readiness to come to the aid of *les miserables* was to remain a marked characteristic of the borough into the distant future.

The practice of "the promenade" has been attributed to the French legacy in Norfolk. This custom, however, was not exclusively French. Throughout continental Europe, even to this day, it is a very popular practice especially in catholic countries such as Spain, Italy, Portugal, and France and also in the

Caribbean islands where it was imported from Europe. In most continental villages the day began early, usually by first light, and the time before noon was spent preparing for the afternoon. Today vestiges of this custom can still be found in small French and other continental European towns and villages away from the hustle and bustle of the larger commercial cities.

Almost all of Norfolk's older communities engaged in the promenade, which became known colloquially as "the evening," before its demise in the late 1960s. Just as on the continent, before noon was the part of the day when housework was done, groceries were bought, bills were paid, yard work was done, and various other tasks were accomplished, especially those related to maintaining one's daily existence and facilitating the events that occurred in the afternoon. Mornings were filled with routine household tasks or going to work, while the afternoons were focused upon getting ready for the evenings—baths were taken, clothes were changed, and dinner was eaten, and then the events of the evening began. In many cases, this consisted of sitting on the porch greeting neighbors as they passed by, strolling along the neighborhood streets as if promenading along the boulevard in one of Georges-Pierre Seurat's paintings, chatting and gossiping, and in some cases playing a game or two of sport in the summer months when the daylight lasted until almost 9:00. If one were of an appropriate age, the evenings were also for courting—properly chaperoned, of course, by a younger sibling or a dutiful aunt. These were magical hours when all the cares and concerns of daily life could be abandoned for moments of relaxation and community. This custom had a particularly genteel feeling, in the sense of promoting the enjoyment of life rather than the sense of being born of privilege.

The French were solid traditional capitalists, which meant that they were primarily disposed to seeking the exchange of goods and services for a profit. Their philosophy of "economic traditionalism" was in strong contrast to the English and Scot view that can be said to be more aligned with the ideology of modern capitalism, which advocated the exchange of goods and services in the *pursuit* of profit—a more rapacious form of capitalism—profits for profit's sake. Fortunately, the French who remained in Norfolk and adhered to their notion of traditional capitalism by opening little shops that sold dry goods, bakery items, or the like, were able in many cases to return to the former levels of prosperity that they had attained in Santa Domingo.

Around this same time another group was making a mark upon Norfolk as well. That group was the newly freed Africans, or free people of color as they were sometimes referred to. The total population of Norfolk around that time according to the 1790 census was 2,957, of which there were 1,622 whites (including ethnic whites such as the French and Spanish) and 1,335 blacks. Within the black population 1,274 were enslaved and 61 were free. Slave holders could free their slaves legally in Virginia in 1782 by a transfer of ownership much the same way one would transfer land or property. The manumission process consisted of an owner making a written declaration at the courthouse describing the enslaved, providing the reasons for the manumit, and renouncing all claims to the person. The deed of manumission was then signed by two witnesses and the formerly enslaved person became legally free.

The number of freed persons grew with each following census: 352 in 1800, 592 in 1810, and 599 in 1820. Yet these numbers represented a very small portion of the African population in the Norfolk area—the greater percentage of Africans was still enslaved. It is not really known whether these numbers represent the actual number of Africans who were freed here in Norfolk or whether they include freed people from other counties who had migrated here. That figure might have also included a fair number of runaways who were able to escape their enslavement and make their way to Norfolk, finding work as laborers on the docks and mixing in with the free African population.

Most often freed Africans were skilled artisans who were able to make a living as cabinet makers, barbers, blacksmiths, and so on. It was also possible to be hired to work on the docks—dock work did not necessarily require skilled labor but there was always something to do and one could usually find work there. The presence of free Africans contributed an interesting economic and religious dynamic to life in Norfolk. Occupationally they were usually doing the work that they were trained to do and were not taking someone else's place. Nevertheless, to some degree their presence in these jobs as free persons posed a bit of cognitive dissonance for European Norfolkians. This would be particularly true in the case of artisans. The enslaved person who regularly cut one's hair might still be cutting one's hair, but now as a free person with many of the same entitlements as the European American client. The presence of freed Africans on the docks was not unusual either. It had been the custom for years for enslaved Africans to hire themselves out to work on the docks. The prevailing attitude was, to some degree, that labor was labor as long as it did not cause a problem. By tacit agreement, an enslaved worker was allowed to hire himself out as long as he gave his salary to his owner minus approximately 10¢. Glancing at African workers on the docks one would have been hard pressed to distinguish between those who were hiring themselves out, those who were enslaved, and those who had been freed.

Nevertheless, newly freed Africans were clearly perceived as a threat to the system of enslavement. However, they were not the most feared—the most feared were the runaway Africans. These workers were still legally someone's property and as such constituted an economic loss for their owner as well as a source of embarrassment at their having been outwitted by their property. The legend of Frank Guy illustrates both the benefits for the enslaved in running away and the resulting loss to the owner. Frank Guy was enslaved on a plantation in Franktown on the Eastern Shore of Virginia. As the story goes, having been a dutiful, conscientious slave, Guy enjoyed the privileges of church attendance, overseeing plantation work, and accompanying his owner to a number of business activities. As a teenager, Guy had determined that he would free himself by running away. His plan took several months to develop and almost a year to fully implement. Because of his position on the plantation and his experience off it, Guy was able to assimilate himself into the mass of Africans in Norfolk without attracting notice. The biggest problem facing him was his lack of the necessary papers that would indicate his freedom if he were questioned. Slaves had to carry a pass when they left their owner's property, and even free Africans had to carry a town clerk's certificate at all times. It is not known exactly how he overcame this obstacle, but it is known that he was literate as a result of having attended Sunday school, so it is assumed that he was able to forge freedom papers and any other necessary documents. It would also not be far-fetched to suppose that at the time there might have been an underground market in forged freedom papers here in Norfolk.

Somehow, perhaps by luck or pluck, Guy was able to become a waiter of some sort. It would be his occupation all his life until his death in 1916 at the age of 90. An examination of his household inventory and his tangible assets at the time of his death reveals his attainment of a lifestyle that only a few of the very well-off could have hoped to achieve during this period. While Guy's story is a testament to the courage and strength of an enslaved person, it was a nightmare for those who benefited from the system of enslavement. The very idea that Guy could escape and elude capture and even prosper was a chink in the armor of a system thought to be impenetrable.

During this same period, Norfolk's population of believers was also expanding and diversifying. It is difficult to imagine today the strength of doctrinal divisions during the 18th century. These differences were often the grounds upon which religious intolerance was justified. The Anglican dominance of official religious life was broken in 1784–1785 by the adoption of Thomas Jefferson's "Statue for Religious Freedom." Needless to say, believers of other denominations had not been dissuaded from forming and worshiping privately. The period from 1793 until approximately 1820 can be viewed as the period of church diversification.

Beginning with the Methodists, who were the first group of believers to organize and build an official church, other groups soon followed. In 1793 the Methodists established a church building on Fenchurch Street. George Tucker in *Norfolk Highlights: 1584–1881* writes, "Since the ground in that area was marshy, the church was built upon blocks eight feet high to protect it from being flooded by the high tides." Tucker goes on to say, "This church served the Norfolk Methodist congregation until February, 1800, when a lot was purchased on Cumberland Street. . . . This property in 1802, known as the Cumberland Street Methodist Church was the mother church of all the Methodist congregations in Norfolk today."

The next to build a church were the Roman Catholics in 1794. Even though the Irish population in this area was relatively small, combined with the French it provided a sufficient number of people to form the basis of a congregation and secure for the believers enough land for the building of a church at the corner of Holt and Chapel Streets. Even though the number of Roman Catholics was small in comparison to other denominations, their numbers grew in time and as a group Norfolk's Catholic churches were able to have an impact in the community. This was due in large part to the church's willingness to join with other Christian believers around a cause.

The Presbyterians were the next group to formally organize and purchase land to build a church. Even though they were one of the oldest groups of believers, they did not appear in a rush to organize nor to build a church structure. Perhaps the reason might be that for over 70 years they were worshiping in the Borough Church under the guise of being Episcopalian, hiding in plain sight, as it were. In "The Case of the Missing Presbyterians," William C. Woolridge writes:

> The solution to the case of the missing Presbyterians is more dramatic than either Armstrong or the academics imagined. Rather than accept the restrictions on dissenters, imposed by the British, the local Presbyterians appear to have co-opted old St Paul's, the established borough church. Presbyterians in Church of England clothing, they carried on routinely until the Virginia Statute for Religious Freedom (1786) made it expedient for them to resume overtly their Presbyterian identity.

In spite of the fact that there were a sizeable number of Scots in Norfolk, they did not immediately establish a Presbyterian Church. Actually, it would take until the turn of the 19th century for a contingent of well-to-do Presbyterians to mount a subscription at $100 a share to underwrite the building of the first edifice for Presbyterian worship in Norfolk. Historical rumor has it that the campaign was so popular even Moses Myers, Norfolk's first and most prominent Jewish citizen, contributed to the campaign. The drive was very successful. By 1802, the church was completed on the corner of Charlotte and Bank Streets. The Presbyterian Church building was one of the most unusual church structures in Norfolk at that time. Its most outstanding feature was a bell that hung in a cupola. The church would forever be known by its bell and be referred to as the "bell church."

The last Christians to organize and build a church were the Baptists, who had been organized in Portsmouth since the late 1790s. Finding the commute across the Elizabeth River to Portsmouth too arduous, Norfolk's Baptists requested a letter of dismissal from the Court Street Baptist Church of Portsmouth. In 1800 the newly formed group began services in a hall on Cumberland Street. By 1805, they began to worship in the Borough Church (Old Saint Paul's Episcopal Church), which was now vacant. The congregation grew, and by 1815 there were approximately 280 members. This arrangement continued until 1816 when as a result of a dispute with the pastorate of the Reverend James Mitchell, the English Baptist minister who was vehemently anti-slavery, a contingent of about 25 European American members withdrew to form a European American–only Baptist church on Cumberland Street. According to the First Baptist Archives Committee's essay in *The Historic First Baptist Church Celebrating Two-Hundred Years of Christ-Centered Ministries to the Community: 1800–2000,* "Prior to the acceptance of the Cumberland Street Baptist Church into the Portsmouth Baptist Association, the original church was referred to as 'Baptists of Norfolk' or 'The Norfolk Baptist Church.' " After the Cumberland Street Baptist Church was constituted and accepted as a member of the Association in 1818, the association referred to the predominately black church, which was the original church, as the "Norfolk First Church" or the "First Church in Norfolk." The original church, which continued to be pastored by the Englishman Pastor Mitchell, became "First Baptist Church of Norfolk." To this day there is an ongoing dispute as to which church is the rightful holder of the First Baptist Church title. It seems that the Cumberland Street Baptist Church applied 60 years later to change its name to First Baptist Church, Cumberland Street, Norfolk, using the name of the street to signify the church's location. With time and a site change the street designation dropped out of the name and the Cumberland Street Church began calling itself First Baptist, Norfolk.

Present-day Norfolk has a sizeable population of Jewish worshipers who represent the three branches of Jewish belief—Orthodox, Conservative, and

Reform. Irvin M. Berent, who has written extensively about the history of Norfolk's Jewish community, notes in *Norfolk, Virginia: A Jewish History of the Twentieth Century*, that by 1900:

> Three synagogues had been established and its congregations delineated: A Reformed synagogue, Ohef Sholom, composed of German-born Jews and their descendants; a Conservative synagogue, Beth El, composed mainly of German-born Jews and their descendants who conserved the more orthodox ritual of German Jewry; and an Orthodox synagogue, B'nai Israel, composed of recently arrived Orthodox Jewish immigrants from Russia, especially Lithuania.

Of course everyone is familiar with Norfolk's most famous and prosperous Jewish resident, Moses Myers, who was the son of Hyman Myers, a shochet, or ritual Jewish slaughterer, from Amsterdam. Myers arrived around 1785 accompanied by his cousin Samuel Myers, the son of Myer Myers the famous New York silversmith. Even though a Jewish cemetery would be established by 1817, it would take until about 1840 to make up a minyan, the 10 Jewish males needed to form a meeting group. According to Berent, in that year, "several Torah scrolls were found in a closet in 'the Fire White Pretentious Dwelling' on Cumberland Street, called 'the Castle.' " Berent also writes that "the early 1840s brought the great wave of German Jews into the country, among the first in Norfolk being Jacob Umstadter who helped establish the first congregation in the area. This congregation, known as 'Chevra B'nai Jacob' or 'the House of Jacob,' began in 1848." However, according to Berent, it was the next congregation in 1848 that obtained the first ordained Rabbi: "It was not until 1869 that the first ordained rabbi, Rev. Bernhard L. Fould of Erie, PA became the leader of 'Ohef Sholom,' the new name taken in 1867 after the congregation was reconstituted after the war." By 1870 the reformation of rituals at this congregation led some members to form a new orthodox congregation, Beth El.

Norfolk's Jewish population comprised the largest group of foreign residents at the beginning of the 20th century. According to the 1900 census, about 100 Eastern European Jewish families, about 500 people, lived in Norfolk. According to Berent the more recent arrivals were merchants, like the older German-Jewish immigrants. As the Germans had done earlier, the so-called "Russian Jews" set up small shops along Church Street dealing in grocery, dry goods, furniture, or saloons while living above the shop. The path of Jewish immigration to Norfolk is in many respects illustrative of the classic immigrant route to the American dream, which became a reality for almost all of the Jewish residents who settled here.

# 4. The War Between the States and its Aftermath: 1860–1910

It is difficult to research Norfolk's role in the Civil War from the written sources of the time primarily because the partisan sentiments were so strong on both sides that even the factual evidence is riddled with prejudice. Nevertheless, this divisive period was one of the major defining moments in American history, affording the opportunity to come together as a nation and clarify the notion of individual good versus group good.

In the spring of 1861 Virginia voted to secede from the Union, becoming the fourth state in the Confederate States of America. Just a few days later the Gosport Navy Yard was torched by Federal troops. The USS *Merrimac*, affectionately dubbed "the Queen of the Navy," suffered extensive damage. Fortunately for the Confederates, enough was left of the original ship for it to be refitted with an iron skin that made it a much stronger and more powerful vessel—an ironclad. By March 1862 it was renamed the CSS *Virginia* and engaged in combat with the Union's ironclad, the *Monitor*. Its refitting was so well done that from all accounts the *Virginia*'s hull was hard to penetrate. Most of the rounds hitting it did no more than slightly dent its skin. It did not take long, however, for the *Monitor* crew to figure out the *Virginia*'s limitations, maneuvering it into shoal water where its deep draft limited its ability to maneuver.

With the *Virginia* out of the way, on May 10, 1862, Union forces recaptured Norfolk by truce. Once Union forces were able to get control of the James River, it became clear to the Confederate forces and the citizens of Norfolk that it was just a matter of time before Norfolk would be under siege by the Union. Rather than be attacked, the Confederate forces evacuated the city. Greeting the advancing Union forces, Mayor Lamb and several council members requested a truce. Not wanting their beloved ironclad to be captured by Union forces, the crew of the *Virginia* blew it up. According to Wertenberger and Schlegel:

> While the Union forces were occupying Norfolk, the Confederates had been engaged in destroying the Navy Yard and the shipping in the river. The dry dock was mined and seriously damaged; machinery was broken up, buildings burned, and valuable stores of tobacco thrown in the river. . . . the scene strongly reminded the spectator of the panorama of the burning of Moscow . . . it made the scene one of terrible grandeur.

With the Union flag flying high atop the portico of the Customs House on Main Street, Norfolk spent the rest of the war an occupied city.

Norfolk's occupation lasted for slightly under two years. As the war raged on around them, the people of Norfolk made every attempt to carry on their lives in spite of many hardships. This proved to be extremely difficult however, since Norfolk's raison d'être has always been mercantile commerce. The city was in shambles, routines were disrupted, people were displaced, and the city was under martial law. Aside from the physical damage to their city, which was considerable, Norfolk citizens were most aggrieved at two indignities they found to be unbearable. The first was the command that they pledge their allegiance to the United States. Norfolkians considered themselves a conquered people and did not believe that they should be required to give allegiance to a conquering power. At every turn they resisted when confronted with the order. The other indignity was having to show respect for and take orders from formerly enslaved Africans, many of whom were now Union soldiers charged with keeping order on Norfolk's streets. According to Wertenberger and Schlegel:

> Norfolk's cup of bitterness was full when the Federal authorities began recruiting the slaves, organizing them into regiments, and using them for garrison duty and for expeditions into the surrounding county. . . . To see Negro soldiers drilling in the streets was bad enough, but to have them arrest some old-school

Southerner, or ransack his house, or stand guard over him in prison, was almost too much to be endured.

Norfolk's years of occupation were spent under the authority of Maj. Gen. Benjamin Franklin Butler and Provost Marshall Gen. Egbert L. Viele, who was in charge of all police functions. Many historical sources describe General Butler as a monster who was vehemently disliked by Norfolkians. Certainly his reputation for intransigence preceded him to Norfolk from his former post in New Orleans. According to his biographer, however, Butler was a more complex and to some degree more interesting man than he is often portrayed. In *Benjamin Franklin Butler: Damnedest Yankee*, Dick Nolan credits Butler with being "one of the brightest generals of his time. In many respects he was also the toughest, since at all times he had to cope with the honest enemies before him and with far less scrupulous enemies to the rear." According to Nolan, Butler was responsible for organizing a prisoner swap that rescued Union soldiers from Confederate prisons in Richmond. But perhaps his biggest contribution to history, in Nolan's view, was his idea to declare all runaway slaves contraband of war, thereby freeing them. Of course neither of these deeds were of benefit to Norfolkians and therefore of no consequence as they formed their opinions of him. Butler remained for the general population of Norfolk a harsh, dictatorial occupier.

During the period of occupation, order was established in Norfolk. Butler's administration was reported to have been orderly and efficient, despite what was thought of him personally. There is some dispute as to whether Norfolkians gave their tacit allegiance to the federal government as a condition for doing business as some historians have suggested. It does seem, however, that the Butler administration turned a blind eye to some enterprises as long as they remained under the radar, so to speak. It was actually to both sides' advantage to get business up and running in the city so that its citizens would not be a complete drain on Union coffers.

Once the war was over, Norfolk was faced with the task of rebuilding its infrastructure and reestablishing its mercantile dominance. And it all had to be done in the context of the new national objectives. Norfolk was no longer responsible only to the imperatives of the state, but to those of the federal government as well. The U.S. government required that before rebel states could be readmitted into the Union, common national objectives needed to be established upon which all the states could agree in order to form a new national whole. This was done by "connecting" each citizen directly to the federal government through a series of initiatives. The first was the Legal Tender Act, which gave control of the currency to the federal government. Second, federal citizenship was extended to all Americans. Third, military service was made compulsory for male citizens by draft. Fourth, direct federal taxation was instituted.

Another federal directive was that each state set up a system of free public education for all its citizens. Norfolk had for about a 20-year period prior to the Civil War (1830–1850) provided tuition-free schooling for poor white males and a few poor white females, although the schools were not coeducational. This system of free education was supported through charitable giving, not through direct taxation. In the main, Norfolk shared the general southern reluctance of taxing for educational purposes. Perhaps because of its agrarian economic roots and class-conscious social system, the idea of universal, government-supported literacy was not meaningful to most southerners. Of course, this did not mean that Norfolk's citizens ignored their religious mandates of literacy in the service of salvation. The central issue was whether everyone should be taxed for it.

There is evidence of what might be called an underground network of both church sponsored schools and tutoring houses from the same period. These opportunities were available to both poor white and black youngsters, although there is no indication that they were instructed together. One famous example came to light during the 30-day incarceration of Margaret Douglas in the Norfolk City Jail in 1853. Douglas and her daughter Rosa established a school in their house for free "children of color" as a result of Rosa's experience tutoring the four children of a prosperous barber, James Robinson. Douglas, who was a South Carolinian, knew that many of her contemporaries ran private tutoring schools in their homes for poor white children and that some others ran tutoring schools for free black children. Based upon her observations, she had no reason to believe that her actions were illegal. Douglas's efforts were so successful that at the time of her arrest she is reported to have had an enrollment of approximately 200 students.

Educating Norfolk's children proved to be more engaging than expected. In spite of Norfolk's Protestant roots, education, and public education in particular, was not a priority. Protestant churches, in sharp contrast to Catholicism, traditionally took on the function of teaching literacy to their congregations. This was done in what came to be known as Sunday school, where congregants learned to read the Bible and, in many cases, to write. Geography was also an element of the curriculum, as students learned to recognize the places where important events in biblical history occurred. Sunday school was ongoing, but its success relied upon its students' regular attendance and interest, which was not always consistent. Another more formal method of establishing literacy was the creation of parish schools. According to Wertenbaker and Schlegel:

> It was the custom in the eighteenth century for the minister to conduct an informal school for the parish children. . . . the parish school was limited to the elementary, "three Rs." It is not clear whether the parish schools preceded the Sunday Schools or whether the Sunday Schools were an outgrowth of the parish school. It is more likely that the parish schools were targeted to children and that Sunday Schools were the equivalent to what they are today, schools for learning about the Bible.

Early in the colonial period, in 1728, Samuel Boush, Nathaniel Newton, and Samuel Smith sought authorization to become school trustees and build a schoolhouse on the lot across from the church. Records indicate, however, that it was not until about 1756 that a teacher was hired and accredited. Moreover, it was not until 1761 that the first official school building was completed. The building of the school and the hiring of the teacher came about many years after the Virginia General Assembly authorized the establishment of schools in 1752. Why it took Norfolk so many years to make this happen is a curious question.

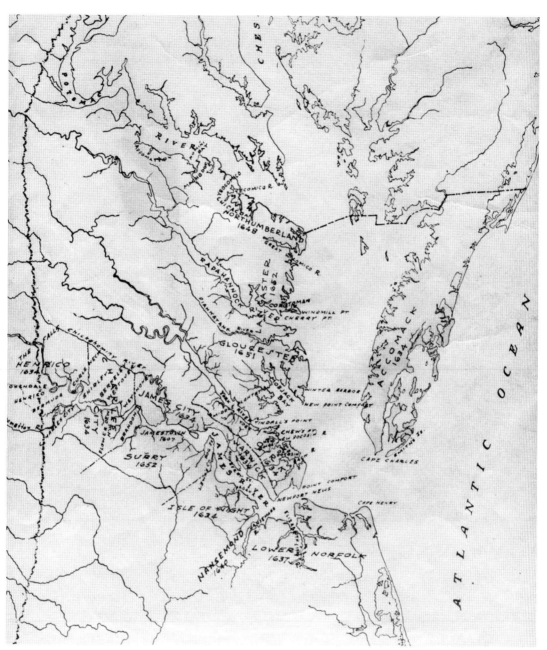

*By 1652 when this map was platted, the settlement had grown to include a great deal of inland territory. Most settlements followed the course of the inland rivers, extending outward from their banks. This pattern was probably adopted as a result of association with the area's indigenous inhabitants, who used the waterways as highways. It is interesting to note that the settlements to the south were less numerous; indeed, there were fewer tributaries in that direction.*

Lord Dunmore was the last royal governor of Virginia. When the Revolutionary War broke out in 1775, he fled to the security of British warships stationed just off the coast of Virginia, where he maintained control over the port until the Battle of Great Bridge dislodged him.

Saintilla Ridgeway, or "Sadie" as she was affectionately known, was the last surviving child of Nancy and Thomas Ridgeway. Sadie's brother died as a toddler. Much of what is known about the Ridgeways and their descendants is due to Sadie's meticulous record keeping of family history. An 1896 graduate from Hampton Normal and Agricultural Institute with a certificate in tailoring, Sadie maintained her craft until she died in her 90s.

Virginia. Norfolk County to wit:

At a Court held for Norfolk County the 16th day of November 1857

The Court doth certify upon the testimony of White persons that Nancy Ann Virginia Elliott child of Josiah Ellet and Jemmima his wife is of mixed blood.

The aforesaid Nancy Ann Virginia Elliott (now Nancy Ann Virginia Young wife of Nelson Young) is of light indian complexion, has a large scar in the centre of the forehead and one on the right wrist—five feet three & a half inches high—was born in the County of Norfolk on the 11th day of October 1836—

I LeRoy G. Edwards Clerk of Norfolk County Court in the State of Virginia do hereby certify that the foregoing is a true copy of the order of said Court and that the description of the said Nancy Ann Virginia Elliott has been correctly made by me.

Given under my hand and the Seal of the said Court this second day of April 1861 in the 85th Year of the Commonwealth

LeRoy. G. Edwards
C.C.

*Though she was born in 1836, Nancy Ann Elliot (later Nancy Ann Young Ridgeway) did not have this birth registration document until November 1857, when she appeared for a court hearing at the age of 21. The document established her free birth, which was important because prior to emancipation it was the custom to re-enslave anyone who did not have official papers attesting to their freedom. By the time she received it she was married to her first husband, Nelson Young, a landowner who was also born free. He died in battle in the Civil War, though it is not known on which side he served.*

*The House of Jacob was the first synagogue structure in Norfolk. It later became Beth El, a conservative synagogue where German Jews and their descendants maintained German orthodox traditions.*

*The Anglican or Episcopal Church was the only church allowed to officially operate in the British colony. Christ Episcopal Church was one of several Anglican churches in Norfolk.*

These three churches represent the establishment
of diverse Christian denominations after the
Revolutionary War, when groups of believers
who had previously worshiped in secret began to
hold public services. Although not the first (the
Methodists established a church in 1793 followed
by the Catholics in 1794), they represent the extent
of religious diversification in the area. The First
Presbyterian Church (above) was established in
1802, followed by a group of Baptists who sought
permission to form their own church in Norfolk
by 1805. Later in the century, two additional
Baptist churches formed from the original church,
Cumberland Street Baptist Church (below) and
Freemason Street Baptist Church (right).

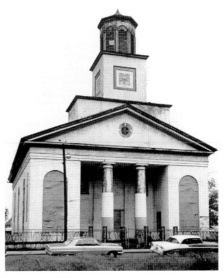

At the time of its founding in 1873, the Leach-Wood Seminary for Girls (above) offered not only the traditional female curriculum with courses in art, music, literature, and social decorum, but also academic subjects such as math, English, Latin, and philosophy. When the school was sold 25 years later—two years prior to Miss Leach's death—the alumna and Miss Wood established an art collection that would serve as a memoriam to Leach. By 1917 the collection had expanded to such a great extent that it outgrew its exhibition space in the Norfolk Public Library. The Leach-Wood Alumni Association, which by then had become the Norfolk Society for the Arts, petitioned city council for land and funds to establish a permanent home for the collection. Pictured below is a rendering of that building, which was named The Norfolk Museum of Arts and Science. One of the museum's most generous donors was Walter P. Chrysler Jr. The museum was renamed in his honor in 1971 and after his death a sizeable portion of his personal collection was bequeathed to the museum. Today the Chrysler Museum of Art has the third largest collection of art glass in the United States.

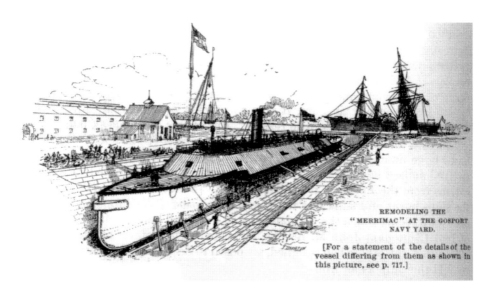

REMODELING THE
"MERRIMAC" AT THE GOSPORT
NAVY YARD.

[For a statement of the details of the
vessel differing from them as shown in
this picture, see p. 717.]

Today it is hard to appreciate the significance of the use of iron in the hull of a battleship.
However, until the Civil War, most vessels were still made of wood. Pictured above is
the Merrimac being refitted to become the Virginia. The refitted "ironclad" is pictured
below engaging the Federal ship Cumberland. The caption on the engraving reads, "The
Civil War in America.—Naval engagement in Hampton Roads: The Confederate iron-
plated steamer Merrimac (or Virginia) running into the Federal sloop Cumberland."

Gen. Benjamin Butler was a controversial figure even before coming to Fort Monroe during the Civil War. His term of office proved to be highly contested, based largely upon the reputation that preceded him from his tenure in New Orleans. Most of Norfolk's citizens were unable to directly challenge his commands and therefore found more passive ways to circumvent them. Nevertheless, some of his initiatives seem progressive in a contemporary context.

The Atlantic City School was one of the four schools desegregated under Major General Butler's command during Norfolk's occupation. However, it did not remain integrated. After the Civil War, all schools were renamed, refurbished, and re-segregated.

*Few people today realize that Norfolk was occupied by Federal troops during the Civil War. Occupation was very distasteful for Norfolk's citizens and many put up a great deal of passive resistance. However, many found ways to prosper during this time and ignore the restrictions placed upon them by General Butler's command.*

**MARKET PA...**

**Not Transferable.**

*Provost Marshal's Office,*

Portsmouth, Va. *June 27th* 1864.

No. *1684*

Permission is hereby given to *Mrs. S. Elliott*

................................................ to come to PORTSMOUTH and

return without molestation or interruption for *4* weeks.

Pass limited to *3* miles, direction of ..............

*Seuls Creek* on *Sylis Creek* Road.

By Order of Brig. Gen. ~~EDWARD A. WILD,~~

*Vogdes*

CAPT. and PROVOST MARSHAL.

"OLD DOMINION" PRINT.

*This market pass was issued to Nelson Young, who was a free African American prior to the Civil War. Nevertheless, he needed a pass to travel between Seouls Point Road and his home. As occupied territory, Norfolk's African American community became equalized: all persons of color had the same restrictions no matter their previous status. This pass was signed by Provost Marshal General Egbert Viele, who was responsible for keeping order and for other police-like functions in occupied Norfolk.*

*Lamberts Point was the industrial part of town, although it had a few family homes too. Coal arrived at the point on Norfolk and Western (today's Norfolk Southern) coal trains from West Virginia and was loaded onto cargo ships for export around the world. Frequently these overloaded train cars provided much needed coal for poorer families. By walking the tracks after a train had passed, a person could pick up enough coal to fill a bucket. Often, one could gather enough coal to supply a family's heating needs for a week. This industry is still active today, and motorists are often stuck for 15 to 20 minutes behind 100-car trains at crossings throughout the city. Princess Ann Road near Tidewater Drive is a particularly challenging crossing. The city has not been insensitive to the problem and has built several underpasses at former crossings to alleviate the traffic tie-ups.*

Perhaps as a result of the outright physical and psychological brutality of slavery, European Americans feared African Americans would use the distraction of war as an opportunity for revenge. However, history has never shown that to be the case. Pictured here is Clarence Bailey, a Norfolk soldier who served very loyally as a first lieutenant in the 368th infantry, 92nd dental division of the U.S. Army in World War I. A self-employed dentist after the war, Dr. Bailey saw action several times in France and described his military training and subsequent service as "a great institution." Two pages of his 1919 military service record are pictured below.

# War Camp Community Service

## INFORMATION

### For Soldiers, Sailors, Marines and the General Public

**INFORMATION**

Booth, Corner Main and Granby Streets. Phone 5374-Norfolk.
Travelers' Aid, Terminal Station, East Main Street. Phone 3500-Norfolk.
C. & O. Dock, foot Brooke Avenue. Phone 6117-Norfolk.
A. C. L. and Southern R. R. Depots, foot York Street.
Ocean View Station Depot.

**MUNICIPAL BUILDINGS**

U. S. Post Office, Corner Plume and Atlantic Streets.
U. S. Custom House, Corner Main and Granby Streets.
Municipal Offices, Armory Building.

**WHERE TO EAT AND SLEEP**

Red Circle Club No. 1—Cafeteria, beds, reading rooms, etc. 114 Atlantic Street.
Red Circle Club No. 2—Cafeteria, beds, reading rooms, etc. 116 W. City Hall Avenue.
Officers' Club—Dining room, beds, reading room, etc. 112 College Place.
Red Circle Merchant Marine Club—Club rooms, beds, etc. 543 W. Bute Street.
Liberty Club (colored)—Cafeteria, beds, reading room, etc. 556 Church Street.
Norfolk Branch Navy Y. M. C. A.—All privileges extended men in the Service. Brooke Avenue and Boush Street.
Salvation Army, Naval and Military Club—Club rooms, beds, etc. Corner Plume and Granby Streets.
Lutheran Brotherhood Home—Dining room, reading room, beds, etc. Boush Street and College Place.
Victory Service Club—Cafeteria and all club privileges. Atlantic and Plume Streets.
Central Y. M. C. A.—Club privileges. Freemason and Granby Streets.
In addition to the above list of places, hotels, numerous boarding, and lodging houses, as well as private homes are available to men in the service. A special registry is maintained by War Camp Community Service, co-operating with other agencies, which makes possible a large list of desirable rooms at reasonable prices. Call 5374 Norfolk (Information Booth) for full information as to rooms.

**POINTS OF INTEREST IN AND AROUND NORFOLK**

Old St. Paul's Church and Yard. Church Street near Holt Street. Open daily to visitors. Take Church Street and Pine Beach cars.
U. S. Army Base. Take Naval Base, Pine Beach, and Newport News cars.
U. S. Naval Base. Take Naval Base, Pine Beach, and Newport News cars.
U. S. Fort Story, at Cape Henry. Take Cape Henry and Virginia Beach cars.
U. S. Rifle Range, at Virginia Beach. Take Cape Henry and Virginia Beach cars.
U. S. Navy Yard, Portsmouth. Take ferries to Portsmouth.
U. S. Naval Hospital, Portsmouth. Take ferries to Portsmouth.
Ocean View and Virginia Beach, Resorts. Take Ocean View, Old Point, and Virginia Beach cars.
Lafayette Park. Take City Park and Riverview cars.
Fortress Monroe. Frequent boat trips, and Old Point cars.
Hampton. Take boats to Old Point, and cars to Hampton.
Jamestown Island. Take Old Dominion boats from Norfolk, or C. & O. R. R. via Williamsburg.
Yorktown. Take vehicles from Williamsburg or Lee Hall.
Williamsburg. Take C. & O. R. R. from Norfolk.
Dismal Swamp. Trips made by small power boats from Norfolk.
Port Norfolk. Take Ghent and Atlantic City cars.

**DOWN TOWN CHURCHES**
(One of Each Denomination)

Baptist. Freemason Street Church, Freemason and Bank Streets, Rev. Sparks W. Melton, D. D., pastor. Services at 11:00 A. M. and 8:00 P. M. Sunday School at 9:30 A. M.
Catholic. St. Mary's Church, Chapel and Holt Streets, Rt. Rev. Monsignor O'Farrell, pastor. Sunday mass at 7:00 A. M., 9:30 A. M. and 11:00 A. M. Vespers and benediction at 8:00 P. M.
Christian. Memorial Christian Temple, Cooke and Tunstall Avenues. Rev. G. Herbert Ekins, minister-in-charge. Sunday School at 9:30 A. M. Services at 11:00 A. M. and 8:00 P. M.
Christian Science. First Church of Christ, Scientist, 207 West Freemason Street, near Boush Street. Services at 11:00 A. M. and 8:00 P. M.
Disciples. First Christian Church, Colonial Avenue and 16th Street, Rev. Charles M. Watson, pastor. Services at 11:00 A. M. and 8:15 P. M. Bible Class at 9:30 A. M.
Episcopal. St. Luke's Church, Granby and Bute Streets, Rev. David W. Howard, D. D., Rector. Holy Communion, 7:30 A. M. Sunday School at 9:45 A. M. Morning Prayer and Sermon at 11:00 A. M. Evening Prayer and Sermon at 8:00 P. M.
Jewish. Ohef Sholom Temple (Reformed), Stockley Gardens and Raleigh Avenue, Rabbi. Rev. Dr. L. D. Mendoza. Services every Friday evening at 8:00 P. M.
Beth-el Temple (Orthodox), 432 Cumberland Street. Services every Friday evening at 8:00 P. M.
Lutheran. First Church, Moran Avenue and Fifteenth Street. Rev. Earnest Roedel McCauley, D. D., pastor. Services at 11:00 A. M. and 8:00 P. M. Sunday School at 9:45 A. M.
Methodist. Epworth Church, Freemason and Boush Streets. Rev. Samuel T. Senter, D. D., pastor. Sunday School at 9:30 A. M. Services at 11:00 A. M. and 8:15 P. M.
Presbyterian. Second Church, North Yarmouth Street, Rev. D. N. McLauchlin, D. D., pastor. Sunday School at 9:30 A. M. Services at 11:00 A. M. and 8:00 P. M.
Salvation Army. 122 Tabot Street, near Main. Services every evening at 8:00 P. M. except Tuesdays. Sundays at 11:00 A. M. and Bible Class at 2:30 P. M.
Union Mission. Building on Main and Nebraska Streets. Rev. H. H. Kratzig, Superintendent. Services every night at 8:00 P. M.

**BOAT AND TRAIN SCHEDULES**

Norfolk to Newport News. By steamer direct. 6:00 A. M., steamer from Old Dominion Wharf, Tuesday, Thursday, Saturday. 7:45 A. M. and 2:30 P. M., steamer from Old Bay Line Wharf, except Sunday. 9:00 A. M., C. & O. steamer from C. & O. Wharf. 12:30 P. M., C. & O. steamer from C. & O. Wharf. 3:45 P. M., C. & O. steamer from C. & O. Wharf. 6:00 P. M., steamer from Old Dominion Wharf.
By Trolley and Boat via Pine Beach: Take car at Main and Granby streets, 55 minutes before time for boat to leave Pine Beach. Boats leave 6:40, 8:15, 9:00, 9:45, 10:30, 11:15 A. M.; 12 noon, and 12:45, 1:30, 2:15, 3:00, 3:45, 4:30, 5:15, 6:00, 6:45, 7:30, 8:15, 9:45, 11:45 P. M.
By steamer direct every three hours, steamer Endeavor leaves Norfolk, Wharf foot City Hall Avenue. 5:00, 8:00, 11:00 A. M.; 2:00, 5:00, 8:00 P. M. Leaves Newport News, Little Boat Harbor Wharf, 6:30, 9:30 A. M.; 12:30, 3:30, 6:30, 9:30 P. M.
Norfolk to Old Point Comfort. 6:30 A. M., steamer leaves Old Bay Wharf, except Sunday. 9:30 A. M., N. Y., P. & N. steamer from N. Y. P. & N. Wharf. 5:45 P. M., Washington steamer, foot Colley Avenue, Atlantic City. 6:00 P. M., N. Y., P. & N. steamer from N. Y. P. & N. Wharf. 6:15 P. M., Baltimore steamer, foot Jackson Street. 6:30 P. M., Baltimore steamer, foot Main Street.
By Trolley and Ferry via Willoughby Spit: Old Point Express leaves Main and Granby Streets every hour on the hour from 7:00 A. M. until 11:00 P. M. daily, making connection with ferry at Willoughby Spit for Old Point Comfort.
Newport News to Norfolk. 4:30 A. M., steamer from Old Dominion Land Co. Wharf, foot 25th Street. (Pier A.) 9:00 A. M., Old Dominion Boat from Pier A. 5:00 P. M., steamer from Old Dominion Land Co. Wharf, foot 25th Street, Monday, Wednesday, Friday. 11:05 A. M., 2:00 P. M., 6:00 P. M., C. & O. steamer from C. & O. Wharf.
By Boat and Trolley via Pine Beach: Take Boat Harbor Car at 28th Street and Washington Avenue, 12 minutes before leaving time for boat at Boat Harbor, foot of Jefferson Street. 6:10, 7:40, 8:25, 9:10, 9:55, 10:40, 11:25 A. M.; 12:10, 12:55, 1:40, 2:25, 3:10, 3:55, 4:40, 5:25, 6:10, 6:55, 7:40, 9:10, and 11:10 P. M.
Old Point Comfort to Norfolk. 2:30 and 5:00 P. M., Old Dominion boat. 6:00 A. M., Baltimore boat. 7:00 A. M., Washington boat. 8:25 A. M., N. Y., P. & N. boat. 6:30 P. M., N. Y., P. & N. boat.
By Ferry and Trolley via Willoughby Spit: Leave Old Point Comfort 20 minutes after the hour from 8:20 A. M. to 9:20 P. M., Saturday and Sunday, last boat at midnight.
Trains Leaving Norfolk Daily. Norfolk Southern (for Raleigh and Newbern), 9:50 A. M. and 8:35 P. M., from Terminal Station. For Elizabeth City and Edenton, 8:05 A. M.
Chesapeake & Ohio (for Washington, Louisville, Richmond and Cincinnati), 9:00 A. M. and 12:30 and 3:45 P. M. For Washington, D. C., 12:30 P. M.
Norfolk & Western (for Richmond, Washington, Chicago, Cincinnati and Columbus), 8:00 and 8:50 A. M. and 4:30, 5:30 and 8:40 P. M.
Atlantic Coast Line (Charleston, Savannah and Jacksonville), 7:55 A. M. daily, and 3:10 P. M. daily except Sunday. 6:00 P. M. daily.
N. Y., P. & N. (Wilmington, Philadelphia and New York), 9:30 A. M., 6:00 P. M. and 8:30 P. M.
Southern Railway (Atlanta, Birmingham and New Orleans), 7:00 A. M. and 7:30 P. M. Foot of York Street.
Seaboard Air Line (Atanta and Jacksonville), 9:05 A. M. and 8:05 P. M. Foot of High Street, Portsmouth.
Virginia Railroad (Roanoke), 9:30 A. M. and 9:30 P. M. Terminal Station.

Above Schedules subject to change.

ASK FOR NORFOLK GUIDE BOOK AND WEEKLY BULLETIN.

*Norfolk went out of its way to accommodate the influx of service personnel arriving daily during World War II. The list above shows all the services available to enlisted men in the city at the time. A much smaller guide was provided for "Colored Servicemen."*

*This couple appears to be dancing the jitterbug at the Colored USO on Smith Street. There were approximately eight USO centers throughout Norfolk, making recreation conveniently available for servicemen and their dates. The Smith Street branch was exclusively for African American service personnel.*

This photograph captures the enthusiasm and attraction that young women had for men in uniform. Not only were families proud of their sons and brothers who went off to the war, but as can be seen here, young misses clamored to be photographed with one of them.

This photograph appears to have been taken at an outdoors USO facility. Notice the hanging lights suspended from the poles. Dances of this sort were held weekly and although nice girls from good families were not expected to attend, many did even if they had to sneak out to do so. This was very much a part of the "rite of passage" into young adulthood.

Rather than risking attack by British naval forces waiting just off the Virginia coast, the German ship Prinz Eitel Friedrich was initially allowed to wait out the early days of World War I in Norfolk. When the United States entered the war on April 17, 1917, however, the ship became a spoil of war and its crew prisoners of war. This photograph shows what became known as German Village. The inscription on the back of the photograph, written by the photographer C. H. Walker, reads "German Raiders Kronprinz Whilem and Kronprinz Eitel Friedrich interned at Navy Yard 4/15/15. After 4/19/17 when the United States declared war, the ships were seized and converted to troopships."

Photographer C. H. Walker's inscription on the back of this photograph of German Village reads, "Three German sailors from the Kronprinz Whilem making model soldiers for sale. At first internees, they became prisoners of war when the United States entered World War I in April, 1917." The crews of the two ships were later transferred to Fort McPherson, Georgia, for the duration of the war.

Unlike the German sailors stuck in Norfolk at the outbreak of World War I, the Japanese who found themselves here on December 7, 1941, the day Pearl Harbor was bombed, were immediately rounded up and contained. This was the act of Norfolk's city manager Charles Borland, who did not wait for a declaration of war. Norfolk's Japanese community—some of whom are pictured here—was quite small at the time, with about 25 to 40 people. Some of them were U.S. citizens. The first photograph depicts the rounding up of the Japanese in one room. The second shows the interrogation process, which appears to have been humane even though we have no idea of the nature of the questions.

*Families of soldiers fighting in World War II often displayed intense patriotism. Not only is the entire front of this Norfolk house draped in red, white, and blue banners, there is also a double blue-star banner in the front window, indicating that two members of the household were serving in the military.*

*While it is unlikely that anyone would call Bishop "Sweet Daddy" Grace a Norfolk custom, he certainly was a Norfolk institution. Charismatic and flamboyant, he was beloved by his devoted followers as well as by many in the general population. His good works were legendary. Bishop Grace built an apartment complex for the needy, fed masses of people who were hungry, and provided a social outlet for many by staging an annual parade down Chapel Street. Hundreds of people from both sides of the tracks lined the street to see the Booker T. Marching Band, the majorettes, and an assortment of other acts and groups.*

*Both the ferry and the streetcar were the chief means of transportation in Norfolk prior to World War II. The influx of military personnel and their families overwhelmed the system, which resulted in the city having to reassess its means of transportation.*

The above photograph of Tom Vourlas and his wife was taken during his retirement. Vourlas's success, which mirrored the success of many of his compatriots in Norfolk, can be attributed to his ability to identify a niche and fill it. Vourlas saw the need for quick, low cost, healthy lunches for railroad workers. Most of his establishments were located near jobsites, which allowed workers to eat, relax, and get back to work all within their allotted breaks. His perserverance allowed Vourlas to achieve the "American Dream," but the achievement he was most proud of was his service to his community and his church, particularly as its cantor. His son Nick is pictured at left with one of his friends in front of his father's restaurant.

*Malonzo Marciano's work and life typify the Fillipino experience in the Hampton Roads area. Born in 1897 on the Philippine island of San Fernando Pampago, Marciano enlisted in the U.S. Navy at 18 and served in various capacities for 22 years. In 1938, he became a civilian employee at the shipyard. At the outbreak of World War II he was recalled to active duty. Six years later, at the end of the war, he again returned to civilian life but remained at the shipyard until his retirement in 1953. Never satisfied with just doing his job well, Marciano engaged his curious mind and explored all the options and experiences available to him during his voyages. His notebooks, pictured below, are full of graphic detail of the sights and sounds he encountered around the world.*

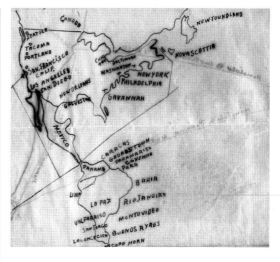

*Customs are important in the south and not even a world war could dampen Norfolkians' enthusiasm for Easter bonnets and new finery. These ladies were photographed on their way home from church in their new Easter chapeaus. Even small children took part in the Easter tradition, as illustrated by these three girls blithely walking along Colonial Avenue in their Easter finery.*

*Easter was also special to this young couple, pictured to the right leaving church. Even small children took part in the Easter tradition, as illustrated by these three girls below blithely walking along Colonial Avenue in their Easter finery.*

*Few Norfolk residents are aware of the existence of the First Chinese Baptist Church, even though it dates from the beginning of the 20th century. Even though the church began in Norfolk, many of its members moved further east, settling in Virginia Beach and the surrounding suburban cities. The church followed its members and relocated to Virginia Beach, where its congregation continues to grow. The church offers services in both English and Chinese and retains two pastors to minister to its linguistically diverse congregants. The Chinese are the largest group of Asians in the Norfolk area aside from the Filipinos, who because of a special arrangement with the federal government immigrated in large numbers after the first and second world wars.*

In Norfolk, poverty spared no race or nationality. The living conditions of the girls pictured to the right and above were typical of Norfolk's poor. A careful examination of the above photograph reveals that the house was once a fine structure, but deterioration and neglect such as this produced some of the most sickening conditions to be found in the south.

*With the award of a federal grant, Norfolk was able to demolish houses such as those pictured to the left and below and construct new housing for the urban poor.*

*Unfortunately, when the old homes were demolished, the new homes that took their place often had the effect of warehousing the poor into urban ghettos where patterns of frustration produced crime and robbed the residents of personal initiative. Nevertheless, Norfolk today has almost no areas that can be called a slum.*

From the inception of public education in the early 1800s, the basic goals for schools have been to educate future citizens, to reduce crime, and to provide equality of opportunity for the labor market. Berkley/Campostella Early Childhood Center is one of the first examples of Norfolk Public Schools' efforts to ensure that all children have a quality early school experience. Pictured here holding one of her students is the principal, Cheryl C. Bunch, whose thoughtful and innovative leadership has made this initiative an overwhelming success.

True to the belief that one cannot be enculturated into the productive norms of society too early, these children are enrolled in the Even Start Program, which takes in pre-preschoolers to help develop their affective and cognitive skills in preparation for preschool.

*The Norfolk Seventeen were the 17 students selected to be the test case against school desegregation in Norfolk. They bore the brunt of the hostilities and frustrations of both sides. Because Norfolk was determined to portray its final compliance as peaceful, they were strongly encouraged to mute their accounts of the subtle and not-so-subtle confrontations that left permanent scars on their psyches.*

*This photograph shows Doumar's drive-in restaurant in 1981. Aside from food at reasonable prices and famous handmade ice cream cones, another major attraction was the roller-skating waitresses carrying trays full of food. Even though the waitresses no longer wear roller skates, the restaurant remains popular and is always full. One of the keys to Doumar's success might be that the prices have increased only slightly over the years while the quality of the food has remained consistent.a*

*Norfolk's economy relied heavily on businesses that took advantage of the city's convenient access to the sea. The boats pictured here are typical of the many working and recreational craft that ply Norfolk's waters. Most local marine businesses are single-owner enterprises with a limited number of employees.*

The caption on the back of the above photo reads, "The Model T touring car was first produced at the Ford Assembly plant in Norfolk on April 20th, 1925." According to the Virginian Pilot the Norfolk plant would become "the largest assembling and distribution plant on the East coast." In its first year the plant assembled close to 30,000 vehicles. By 1928 Ford introduced the Model A and the Norfolk plant workers had to scramble to keep up with demand. In the photograph below Ford plant executives pose with the one-millionith car produced at the plant. The plant's contribution to the local economy has been considerable over its 82 years in Norfolk. Its scheduled closing in 2008 has caused a great deal of anxiety and sadness to the local community and to many of its workers whose families have worked there for generations.

*The Ford Motor Company was not the only national company to locate a plant in Norfolk. The Milwaukee Brewery, Anheuser Bush, also had an operation located in Norfolk. As this photograph shows, it was a rather sprawling affair that represented a sizeable investment by the company. The plant was built near the water, which provided easy transportation to other regions for domestic sales.*

*This early 20th-century photograph of the Jakeman Building gives some indication of the variety of economic opportunities that existed in Norfolk at the time. The building housed the Jakeman jewelry store and shared the other floors with small family-run businesses.*

SCHOOL DAYS

1941-42

*Because of its thriving mercantile trade, Norfolk has always been a magnet for upwardly mobile new residents from all around Virginia and the surrounding states. The couple pictured here are typical of the thousands who moved to Norfolk for increased opportunities. Oliver Clayton Francisco and Mildred Jackson were high school sweethearts in Medowview, Virginia. Even before they married on June 30, 1945, Oliver had determined that he would seek his fortune in Norfolk. While still in high school, he took a summer job with the National Youth Administration here. Upon graduation in 1943, he secured a full-time job with Norfolk and Western Railroad through a relative, but was drafted instead. Wounded in the Battle of Iwo Jima, he returned home and took advantage of the G.I. Bill to earn a college degree in civil engineering from Emory and Henry College. The Francisco family finally moved to Norfolk in 1952, living first in the Brambleton section of the city and then at one of the housing developments constructed for service personnel and base employees' families. The family remained at Broad Creek Village until 1958 when they purchased their own home in Hyde Park, where they live today.*

*The popularization of the bicycle as a mode of transportation in the late 19th century was at least partially responsible for the rise in various woman's movements around that time. The three women pictured above were photographed in Norfolk around the turn of the 20th century.*

*This 1978 photograph of Norfolk's Elizabeth River waterfront captures the beginnings of the Downtown waterfront development. While some of the buildings in the background are still there, this entire section extends along Waterside Drive from Saint Paul's Boulevard on the right to Main Street on the left. One of the most noticeable improvements is the development of Town Point Park in the area to the right of the crane. Each weekend from April through November, Town Point Park serves as the gathering place for various festivals. A multipurpose retail center called Waterside was also developed at the same time as the park. It was to be modeled after Baltimore's famous and very successful harbor development, but because intangible aspects of life vary from city to city, Waterside's success waned after its novelty wore off and the development never quite lived up to expectations.*

*It is hard to imagine that the waterfront area of downtown Norfolk just north of the Battleship Wisconsin was ever this bleak. With the development of downtown living options shown in this 1982 photograph, Norfolk demonstrated its awareness of the advantages of its location on the Elizabeth River for more than commercial trade. The College Place Condominium was one of the first downtown residences of its type. The building juts out over the river and is designed to give all residents a view of the water and sunsets. Many residents were afraid that further development would destroy this advantage; however, the permanent docking of the Wisconsin as a naval museum and the building of another set of condominiums on the opposite finger extending out onto the river has only enhanced the beauty of the waterfront and added to the sense of exclusiveness that waterfront property provides. Of course Norfolk is a city of trade and its waterfront is far too valuable to allow it to serve only recreational and residential purposes. To capitalize on that value, the city is building a passenger terminal for its considerable cruise ship business on the other side of the Wisconsin just beyond the Maritime Museum. It is anticipated to be ready for passenger use by late 2007.*

Although not often thought of as a method of education, there was a much more popular way for poor and enslaved boys to become literate, which was through the system of apprenticeship. When first adopted in 1646, apprentice programs did not have a literacy component. For the most part, apprenticeships were seen as a way to learn a trade and provide a service to commerce and community. But by 1705, a master was required by law to not only train an apprentice but also provide basic education in reading, writing, and arithmetic. This had the odd side effect of providing rudimentary literacy to the skilled and semi-skilled classes. By 1805 this provision of required literacy as a condition of training was eliminated—someone had noticed.

Most scholars have asserted that unlike the north where the population was a mixture of Europeans who spoke different languages, worshiped in different ways, and observed different customs, the south was ethnically homogeneous—the European population at least—and there was little need nor desire to use education as a means of "social control" and "cultural transmission." To some extent this is true; however, the differences in educational objectives between the regions are far more complex than they may at first appear. Education is not neutral—schools are set up in a society to transmit the society's culture along with knowledge. It is through school that children learn the values, rituals, history, and accepted behaviors of their culture. Schools of course share this responsibility with the home and the church, but it is the task of the school to teach the public manners that prepare the child to interact with the larger world.

Unlike the northern colonies, which had a high number of immigrants from Ireland and other parts of Europe that the English believed to be less civilized and in need of conversion, Virginia, and Norfolk in particular, was relatively homogeneous culturally. The need to establish schools to bring a group in line with the British way of life was far less pressing in this region. The British certainly felt the need to control the indigenous peoples, but as history informs us, they would not be controlled. Records indicate that the Virginia Company required each town to educate the Indian children in their area in religion and "civilized living." Plans had already been drawn up for establishing a college in Henrico City near Richmond for Indian boys and one in Charles City for European American boys. But the massacre of 1622, in which the Powhatan attacked the English settlements on both sides of the James River and left approximately 400 men, women, and children dead, nullified plans for any form of schooling for indigenous children. Social control, cultural transmission, and religious conversion would henceforth have to be achieved by the force of a gun.

There had always been some interest in establishing a grammar school for privileged boys in Norfolk. One of the important structures burned during the Revolutionary War was the old grammar school across from the borough church. By 1786 it was rebuilt and renamed the Norfolk Academy. The Academy offered a classical curriculum, which consisted of the study of Latin, Greek, and French, along with English grammar, reading, writing, arithmetic, bookkeeping, and geography. Upperclassmen wore a black band extending from the right shoulder to underneath the left. Lowerclassmen were distinguished by blue ribbons in their lapels. In 1841 with John Scott as the headmaster, Norfolk Academy was rebuilt and reestablished on Bank Street, where the building remains.

From about 1815–1850 Norfolk had its own Lancastrian school. The idea behind the Lancastrian method was that large numbers of students, often poor ones, could be taught basic subjects in a systematic way while at the same time learning lessons in moral character development. Classrooms were large, with anywhere from 50 to 500 students. The teacher sat on a raised platform at the front of the room above several rows of monitors, more advanced students who assisted by teaching their row of students the lessons they received from the teacher. The Lancastrian system was a sort of educational factory, in which children of modest means could be instructed cheaply and the values of submission, order, and industriousness could be instilled.

Until relatively recently, education was not routinely provided for girls. Any kind of education they received was through private sources or through the kindness of "lady tutors" who frequently instructed a few girls in the domestic arts in their homes. It was thought that girls did not need the same education as males since their influence was limited to the home and they were expected to rely upon their husbands for guidance and support. This kind of thinking persisted in Norfolk and throughout much of the country well into the 20th century, but there were exceptions. The creation of the Leache-Wood School and the Norfolk College for Girls in 1873 provides a good example of what might be called progressive thinking for that time. At these schools, girls learned traditional subjects such as English, mathematics, and Latin while also studying literature, art, and music appreciation. By 1880 another school for girls opened in Norfolk, the Norfolk School for Young Ladies. Just as its name implies, it featured courses that were appropriate for the refinement of young girls into young ladies. It was later replaced by Mary Washington College, which continued its mission.

Even though the Virginia General Assembly authorized the establishment of a free public school system in 1850, it took Norfolk another eight years to open four public elementary schools for white children. All children between the ages of six and twenty-one were eligible to attend one of the four elementary schools. Thomas Tabb became Norfolk's first public school superintendent. At the beginning of the Union's two-year occupation of Norfolk in 1863, General William Butler ordered that public elementary schools be open to all children in the city. Norfolk parents were horrified at the thought of racially integrated schooling and withdrew their children from the four elementary schools. The parents' resistance was also due in part to their disdain for General Butler, a Yankee, and with being occupied. Nevertheless, the schools became open to all black students who wished to attend. In many ways this was a social class issue and not a racial one. Prosperous parents who did not wish for their children to attend integrated public schools sent them instead to the various private schools established for that purpose. Norfolk's citizens could not have known that this situation would presage their response to school integration some 90 years later during the civil rights era when the state of Virginia imposed an order of "massive resistance" on Norfolk's public schools. Meanwhile, with the Civil War over, Norfolk parents still would not consider the idea of integrating the public elementary schools, so another solution had to be considered.

In the war's aftermath, education became one of the tools of reconstruction. As a result of the Emancipation Proclamation, Virginia, and Norfolk in particular, had to use schooling as a way to socialize former slaves into the

American way of life and to instill values and ideas that would help the newly freed Africans find their place in society. But the four public elementary schools available to them during the occupation reverted back to being only for European American children once the war was over. So the question of how to educate newly emancipated Africans became the province of the Bureau of Refugees, Freedmen, and Abandoned Lands, popularly known as the Freedmen's Bureau. This agency, set up by the federal government in 1865, was created in part for that very reason. However, even though the Bureau oversaw the creation of a number of schools throughout the south, the responsibility to staff, run, and ultimately fund many of the schools eventually became the task of religious organizations.

One notable effort in Norfolk was the creation of a high school by the United Presbyterians. (The Norfolk Presbyterians also set up a school for newly emancipated youngsters at 919 Cleveland Street under the superintendence of George H. Brown for approximately one year.) In 1882, by an order of their general assembly, the northern branch of the United Presbyterians founded Norfolk Mission College in Norfolk as a part of their mission outreach. The idea was to set up a school that would charge a small tuition to those who could pay and admit free those who could not, thereby admitting all students who wanted to attend. Even though the school charged some of its students tuition, it was considered the first privately funded public school for African Americans in Norfolk. The purpose of the school was "to prepare young men and young women so thoroughly that they may be a power in the uplifting of their own people." Norfolk Mission College stood out among peer institutions because of its commitment to provide a comprehensive education in the classical humanist style.

Hampton Normal and Agricultural Institute, just a little over 20 miles on the other side of the bay, was established in 1867 right after the Civil War. Hampton initially, however, was not designed to provide a classical education. It was set up to train elementary school graduates who, upon completion of the two-year program, would receive a common teaching certificate that would allow them to become teachers in elementary schools. Often normal schools tended to attract older, less academically prepared students who were economically challenged. Training in manual labor was at the core of the normal school curriculum of teacher training. The school appealed to many of Norfolk's African American families because it was nearby, and because it afforded the opportunity to move easily to the top of the post-war pecking order. While there was much debate about the types of education that would be appropriate for former slaves, Hampton Institute's president, Samuel Chapman Armstrong, advocated educating them in labor skills and rudimentary literacy so that they could assume roles in the labor market. Students could also be trained to teach the trades and elementary education, thereby providing a body of African teachers for African students.

In establishing Norfolk Mission College, the Presbyterians were asserting their belief that the answer to the problem of full employment for Africans was in a classical-liberal curriculum that contained some training in vocational subjects. This would allow them to be in the best position to select where they wished to be positioned in the labor market. These notions were very progressive for the time. In *The Education of Blacks in the South, 1860–1935*, James D. Anderson wrote:

> The missionary philanthropists . . . support classical liberal education for Black Americans as a means to achieve racial equality in civil and political life. They assumed that the newly emancipated blacks would move into mainstream national culture, largely free to do and become what they chose, limited only by their own intrinsic worth and effort. . . . It was supposed axiomatically, in other words, that the former slaves would be active participants in the republic on an equal footing with all other citizens. Education, then, according to the more liberal and dominant segments of missionary philanthropists, was intended to prepare a college-bred black leadership to uplift the black masses from the legacy of slavery and the restraints of the post-bellum caste system.

While this debate was raging, Norfolk was also struggling with its educational objectives for its white students. Even though there were approximately 3,500 students eligible to attend Norfolk's four elementary schools, only one-third were enrolled. The elementary schools offered a basic elementary education, which was not regarded as necessary nor important to the needs of the larger segment of Norfolk's white population. This ambivalence towards education among the basic working segment of the population had a great deal to do with the availability of jobs. Norfolk has always been a place where one could find a job, particularly a labor intensive job. Nevertheless, by the time the first high school for European American children was established in 1894, the curriculum was based upon the classical-liberal model and remains so today.

This brings into focus Norfolk's attitude about education and place. Norfolk was never a town of great upward social mobility. Because of its small-town localism, Norfolkians always seem to have only a few degrees of separation between themselves and anyone who they needed to know. In fact, one could say that social class in Norfolk was both prescribed and static—no one in, no one out. To some extent, this remains true of the social core today.

Norfolk had always been a welcoming harbor for people from other countries, particularly if they were from some part of Europe and could contribute to the local economy. In fact in the early part of the 20th century, there was a move to make Norfolk an official receiving site for immigrants. The idea was, it seems, to relieve New York and Baltimore of some of their congestion by establishing an alternate port of entry to the United States in Norfolk. This would have greatly increased Norfolk's Eastern European population, who would most likely have fit well into the commercial life of the city. According to Berent's *Norfolk, Virginia: A Jewish History of the Twentieth Century*, "If Norfolk was to become the New York of the South, it would have to have its own facilities like Ellis Island for receiving immigrants. In an effort to push this idea, a conference was held in Petersburg in May, 1907." Berent notes that there were representatives from Norfolk at the meeting in Petersburg. According to the *Ledger-Dispatch* of May 18, 1907, "it was further said that facilities for inspecting and caring for the immigrants must first be provided, a thing which may easily be done by the government, which at Ellis Island constructed, at the cost of the people, such piers and buildings as required." According to Berent, in spite of the incorporation of the Southern Immigration Association in Norfolk in 1907:

> The dream of Norfolk becoming an immigration center remained only a dream. . . . There is nothing in the way of immigrants landing here, this being a port of entry and there being here an office of the United States Immigration Service. . . . The North German Lloyd Steamship Company . . . recently established a passenger agency here and it is believed that were such concerted effort made as has been described the company will bring immigrants here.

The interest in Norfolk as a port of entry continued until 1925, when the government began placing quotas on immigrants.

Despite their best efforts at lobbying for 18 long years, the Southern Immigration Association and its supporters were unsuccessful at creating an "Ellis Island of the South" in Norfolk. Nevertheless, the city continued to welcome people from certain countries and from certain economic classes. It became the place for groups who could fit in and maintain their ethnic customs, habits, beliefs, and religious practices behind the veil of segregation.

# 5. THE CUSTOMS OF A MODERN CITY: 1910–2006

The period after World War II can be seen as a time of transition from the sleepy southern city of the pre-war years to the energetic post-war years. It was a time of redevelopment, integration, and modernization in both the material conditions of the city and also in its customs. Norfolk remained an identifiable southern city well into the 1960s in spite of its commitment to commerce and the large presence of the U.S. Navy, which prompted Norfolk to make major improvements. The sudden influx of sailors and their families during and after the war necessitated that Norfolk bring its infrastructure, its housing, and its transportation systems up to date, among many other improvements. Because of the lack of affordable housing, the Norfolk Housing Authority, which was created in 1940 to address Norfolk's need for slum clearance, focused its attention on providing temporary housing for military personnel. In an effort to alleviate the housing crunch, the authority created Merrimack Park with federal funds. It contained 500 living units, a community center, and an administration building, which included an auditorium for live entertainment, along with offices and utility space.

The Navy can justly claim responsibility for updating Norfolk's transportation system. Not all service personnel had cars and many of them needed to rely on public transportation to get to their military jobs. It was not uncommon, according to Wertenberger and Schlegal, to see "a streetcar with five or six sailors on the roof or hanging on outside the rear platform. One sailor swore that he never knew that cars had seats." Norfolk responded to the overcrowding with increased street lights, street improvement, and ultimately major improvements to the city's infrastructure funded by the federal government enabling motorists to move about the city in a timely and efficient manner. Also, for some time Norfolk's water system had not been adequate. Again with government assistance, Norfolk was able to improve its water supply and provide enough water for the Navy and local residents.

Even though the Navy had a very large presence in Norfolk, its members actually had difficulty penetrating the local culture. Good families were reluctant to allow their daughters to socialize with Navy men unless of course they were commissioned officers, in which case status outweighed social class. According to Marvin Schegel in *Conscripted City: Norfolk in World War II*, "For the enlisted men, segregation was almost as complete as for the Negro. No 'nice' girl was allowed to go out with a sailor. Most civilians accepted the popular conception of the peacetime Navy that a man who enlisted was probably a failure as a civilian and had no decent moral standards."

Reflecting on how things used to be, neighbors in one of Norfolk's older sections, Lambert's Point, recounted an oft-told tale about a respected family with six daughters that illustrates the interaction between community and private life. As the story goes, during the war years, it was not unusual to see the daughters of this family keeping company with "white hats," which was the colloquial term for sailors. To see good girls keeping company with sailors was alarming to the neighbors because in those days neighbors' children were as carefully monitored and cared for as one's own. Since sailors had never been very high in Norfolk's social pecking order, ranking only slightly above laborers even during colonial days, they were considered by the neighbors to be unsuitable for proper young ladies. So when one of the family's daughters married a Navy man, the only consolation for the community was that he was not a white hat but a "braid," or officer. The term referred to the decoration on an officer's hat.

Another contributing factor to this attitude was that the Navy population was viewed as transient, placing most Navy families and servicepeople on the surface of Norfolk society. It was not that Norfolk's established community did not appreciate the Navy's efforts on their behalf, nor that they did not like the improvements the federal government's money provided, they were just reluctant to acknowledge the equality of "foreigners" from outside their community, even if they were fellow Americans. This xenophobic, old south attitude was very prevalent in Norfolk. Most people were classified as being either from "here" or from "there." If one was from there, then one was always a bit suspect; if one was from here, then one's actions and attitudes were predictable. One of the very first questions that a Norfolkian would ask when being introduced to someone new was whether the person was from outside of or from inside of the community. Frequently the first question was, "where are you from or what neighborhood are you from?" and then the next would be, "who are your people?" Even though few Navy families or personnel penetrated Norfolk's old guard, Navy people found life satisfactory enough to remain here and set up residence after the war was over.

Well into the 1970s, daily life in Norfolk retained many aspects of its agrarian pre-industrial past. Its southernness was apparent in its laws, government, and customs. Southerners have always been known for their indirectness in speech and action—speaking around a purpose or asking or doing by suggestion—and Norfolkians were no exception. Well-bred Norfolkians shied away from using words and terms that they regarded as too harsh or coarse. The idea, it seems, was to avoid terms that provided graphic descriptions. One would instead substitute more generalized terms that alluded to the desired description, thereby softening the effect. The use of euphemisms was very popular. A woman who was pregnant would be spoken of as "with child," which shifted the focus of the discussion from the process of conception, which one would never publicly discuss, to the result of it. To call a person fat was just plain insulting in its harshness. Someone who would be fat in the north would be described as "plump" instead. It was acceptable to refer to children by their gender, "boy" or "girl," rather than their names. However, it was very demeaning to refer to full grown men and women by these terms. This practice was used widely to punctuate the perceived status of adult African Americans or occasionally to refer to European American adults of lower social rank. The condition of hysteria, which seemed to occur abundantly in the south according to the female characters in Tennessee Williams's plays, was referred to as "nervous" or "high strung."

Indirect action, unlike indirect speech, relied much more on the process of enculturalization. It was easy for someone not raised in a particular culture to miss the point of what someone was doing, or rather not doing, and which was intended to communicate a message. When a young lady had a gentleman caller, for example, and her father decided to go upstairs for the night even though it might have been early, he would gather up his things and go to the daughter and her visitor and let them know that he was going upstairs. This was an unspoken message to the young man to leave, no matter the time or whether or not the girl wanted him to stay. There would be no way for anyone not reared in southern culture to know this because the father would never articulate it—southerners feel that a person should just know some things by the process of being reared and socialized by their parents.

People who were older or had a higher social rank than oneself were almost always referred to with a Miss or Mister attached to their surname, or to their first names as a form of endearment. This is much like the Japanese custom of attaching the suffix -san to the end of a person's name as a sign of respect. In the south and in Norfolk in particular, affection for friends was indicated by assigning a special nickname to that person. Nicknames were very descriptive and frequently followed one throughout life. Another rather striking feature of southern speech was the use of the childhood name for a parent, no matter how old the child became. The most common name for one's mother in Norfolk was Mumma while one's father was referred to as Daddy. And of course everyone was familiar with the terms Sir and Madam as a form of address for strangers.

Another example of Norfolk's traditional southern customs involves dating. The concept of dating is so universal now that it is easy to assume that it is a natural, long-standing process. However, the concept of romantic marriage and the getting-to-know-you ritual of dating really never took hold in our society until the early part of the 20th century. In Norfolk and other parts of the south it was known as "courting," an interesting ritual that had very specific goals. It was not just a way for two young people to get to know each other, but rather involved many more people and required the approval of various members of the society as well as the family.

There are still some versions of the courting ritual around now, though it has been updated for modern times. The original ritual had several stages and it was important that none be skipped. The first stage relied upon a third party as a go-between. One's friend would talk to the person of interest if they knew them personally, or discreetly inquire about them to others if not. This "background check" was not so difficult in Norfolk, where most people were identified by their neighborhood, religious affiliation, and social circle. If the results of the first stage were favorable, an introduction would be arranged. This formality was observed even if the two people had already met informally. The arranged introduction was important because it established an appropriate context for the couple's meeting. It was also important that the introduction take place in an appropriate location, with proper surroundings, such as a party at a friend's house or a prearranged "chance" meeting. Even though the introduction itself was brief, it would last long enough to establish a context for later conversation between the potential couple as well as a basis for an official date to be requested later.

Once the couple had met, a "check out" date was requested by the young man. Usually this was with other people; it was seldom done alone. It could take the form of attending a house party, going to the movies with friends, or going to a football game or coffee with friends. The point was to see the person in a social setting and establish how both parties comported themselves in a group situation. These and subsequent dates all began the same way. The young man called on the young lady at her house, which involved coming inside, sitting down, and meeting her parents and any other members of the family or even friends who might be visiting. The process of picking up the date might take half an hour. Before the late 20th century, a chaperone would have gone on the date with the couple.

Having the first few dates with friends provided an opportunity for them to observe the date's behavior, dress, and manners and offered a relatively safe experience for the young couple. After several successful group dates however, the couple would graduate to a date alone, which was expected to be much more serious and romantic. This was certainly the case for one Norfolk centenarian, Miss CeCe, who as a young maiden in 1936 wrote a poem to her fiancé to express her dissatisfaction with his behavior on a date alone. Some background on the situation may help explain, if not excuse, the young man's actions.

In the Democratic primary in the spring of 1936, the very popular two-term incumbent congressman Colgate Darden was challenged by Portsmouth mayor

Norman R. Hamilton. Darden was thought to be a shoo-in, so it was something of a shock when he lost to the challenger, thereby losing his party's nomination. This bold defiance to a popular incumbent was of particular interest to many and was very much the talk of the town during the first week of May 1936 when the couple went for a Sunday afternoon drive in the country and parked in what was then a kind of lover's lane. Miss CeCe explained recently:

> Politics was fine and I was concerned about who would represent us too. But I did know the difference between civic responsibility and romance. So when I returned home from our outing to the country, or what you young people today call a date, I was very dismayed by my boyfriend's constant discussion of politics. It occurred to me that if he put politics before romance now while we were dating, then he would more than likely put it before romance when we got married. This wasn't my idea of what I thought marriage should be. This is the reason why I decided to break off the engagement then. I didn't want to marry a man who was more interested in politics than in me.

When the young maiden returned home that evening, she gave the situation a great deal of thought and sat down at her desk to write a poem to express her displeasure and her reason for calling off the engagement:

"Down with Politics"

You may talk about your fancies, of your hobbies, whims and such,
Or your various disappointments and of things which bring disgust,

There is nothing I can mention which has me in such a fix,
As the Darden-Hamilton campaign and that work called POLITICS.

Take a moonlight night for instance when you're on a lonely road;
where the stillness is only broken by the croaking of the toad.

When the stars up in the ether seem to twinkle from above
And reveal some hidden message of a Lover to his Love

All at once some words are spoken, but they're
words which give you pain.
For your lover only whispers, "What about Darden's Campaign?"

There are times you feel romantic; full of laughter,
joy and bliss
Want an arm about your shoulder, and a long
endearing kiss

So you cuddle somewhat closer for you're really
in your sins,
Just to hear your boyfriend utter—"Dear I know
he's bound to win."

Wish I had the power given to
me just to help make all the laws

For I'd put in every one I phrased a non-election
clause
I'd name the men for president, for congressmen
or clerks
And say "Now men go to your posts and just begin to work"
There'd be no voting at the polls or scratching out some names,

Both Darden and Hamilton would be liked by all the same

We wouldn't have to worry then about our man
being licked

For all around I'd hang up signs—

DOWN WITH POLITICS!!!

While the poem clearly expresses Miss CeCe's dissatisfaction with politics, it does not indicate in any way her decision to terminate the relationship. When asked, her response was that her fiancé knew how she felt and that the relationship was off without her having to put it directly. She went on to explain that he was shocked and promised to be more attentive to her than to politics. From then on, he came courting with flowers, candy, perfume, or some other trinket for her indulgence.

Up until about 30 years ago, Norfolk was still in the service worker era, when a large number of people earned their living doing domestic labor, farm and yard labor, manual labor, or general contracting. This was a vestige of Norfolk's agrarian and urban enslavement past. Past customs were also maintained to some degree because people still lived in extended communities where there was always someone home to tend to the house and its duties even if the woman of the house had an outside job. Even though Norfolk was never a plantation society, the employment of service workers on a daily basis has always been inexpensive and convenient. Prior to the 1970s, the lack of an abundance of skilled employment opportunities combined with restrictive hiring practices and segregated social conditions confined many people to certain kinds of jobs, which were usually at the lowest end of the employment scale. These prospects led many young people to aspire to domestic service positions, where they could spend their careers in the pay of a benevolent, paternalistic employer.

The account of one such experience reveals how someone faced with a lack of choice responded and made a good, productive life out of the constraints placed upon her in a segregated society. Looking back on her long career as a "shop girl," one Norfolk octogenarian remembered:

> After having graduated from high school, my mother enrolled me in Elizabeth City College in Elizabeth City, North Carolina. Mother believed that by sending me away to school, I'd gain experience in knowing how to carry myself when away from my family and friends. She felt that being away would mature me. She wanted to make it possible for me to get the college education she never had so that I could be independent and support myself in life if I needed to. Perhaps I'd become a teacher or home economist which was all the rage back then. Both of them were very well respected professions for women at that time. Because mother was a domestic worker, she wanted more for me. Well,

like many young people, even today, I didn't have any particular vision for my future. So after having completed my freshman year, I announced that I wouldn't go back for my sophomore year. Mother never registered any disapproval nor did she lecture me nor damn me to an afterlife of hell. She only asked me if I'd something I wanted to do and of course, I didn't. From September through March, Mother allowed me to lounge around the house and engage in whatever teenage activity I enjoyed. But by the end of March, Mother announced that I'd have to find a job. Well, I wasn't quite sure about that but I agreed to go looking for one the following week. On Sunday, Mother presented me with a job advertisement and instructed me to go on Monday morning to apply for the position. When Monday morning came around, I tried to hesitate and delay going to apply for the job. Mother, who anticipated my reaction, awakened me early, prepared my breakfast, provided my carfare and laid out my clothes; yes, that was the custom in those days—to select one's child's clothes even if the child was a young adult.

The job was for a position as a shop-girl in a fancy woman's store downtown. My duties were to dust, clean, and serve the customer's whims. I got the job and was to begin right away— the following day, as a matter of fact. Shortly after being there for a few months, I decided to take a weekend off to go on a trip with my friends. On Friday as I was preparing to go, I announced that I wouldn't be in on Saturday. Well, my boss was certainly surprised, and might even have been amused. He asked me who was going to do my work if I wasn't there? I told him that this was not slavery time and I did not have to ask to be off. But if he was not satisfied, he could call my mother and let her know whether I should come in on Monday or not. By the time I got back from my trip on Sunday night, my boss hadn't called to tell me not to come back to work so I went in on Monday morning as usual. I continued behaving in this way throughout the 40-some years I worked in the shop. When it suited me I spoke up, even when, at times, what I said was probably out of order for my position there. Nevertheless, as time went by I gained more experience and my boss and I formed a warm relationship as employer and employee. As I took on more and more responsibility, I was able to do more jobs, serving as the behind-the-scenes manager and sometimes bookkeeper. No matter how much more responsibility I was given, I was always required to wear my gray and white uniform and black shoes. Yes, I did say something to my boss about it. You know I did, as sassy as I was in those days. But he seemed to believe that because it was the custom in the south for colored girls to wear uniforms, the customers who came into the shop would take offence at seeing me in dress clothes. As he explained it, I would be stepping out of my place. So I continued, for the entire 40 years I was there and no matter how much I advanced, to wear the black shoes and the gray and white uniform of a maid.

I know lots of girls who've had working experiences like mine. We all came along during that time when business was done on a handshake, and personal service was an art. Of course, there was no money to be made. But if one knew how and conserved and saved like I did, then a job like mine could be all right. You know, there was no pension and in some cases there was no social security. There was only a paycheck for the number of hours you worked.

I didn't have a plan when I was a teenager, but I got a plan later. I realized that I would have to provide for myself even if my husband made a lot of money from his work in construction. All things considered, I think we didn't do too badly. We're old now but still able to take care of ourselves. With things being so expensive nowadays, we do worry sometimes that we might run out of money. Well, until that day comes we're doing okay.

Customs, which can sometimes seem almost like rituals, are very dear to Norfolkians. They revere them, guard them, and preserve them long after their function has expired or new ones have been invented to take their place. True to their southern roots, Norfolkians observed the more than 100-year-old custom of assigning each day of the week a specific household activity long into the 20th century. They only gave it up when employment outside the home became so prevalent that it became almost impossible for the family to maintain the schedule. This tradition was so entrenched in the culture that there were dish towels, handkerchiefs, and pot holders with the days of the week and their chores embroidered on them. Children were even taught a song, *Here We Go Around The Mulberry Bush*, which outlined the chores for the days of the week and served as a great way to reinforce domestic socialization. The routine varied by social class, economic income, and individual family patterns. One variation was to begin the week with "Blue Monday," when nothing was scheduled except perhaps collecting the trash. Sunday's leftovers were abundant and no food was prepared. Usually there were no complaints, since it was an opportunity to finish up that last piece of fried chicken, ham, or pot roast that had served as the main course for Sunday's feast.

In many households, however, Monday was for laundry. Washing has always been a major activity throughout the south, but here in Norfolk it took on mammoth proportions. Cleanliness, which was next to Godliness, meant that everything had to be kept spotless. This entailed the use of a product called bluing, which has been in use since 1883. While it is now sold under the name Mrs. Stewart's Liquid Bluing, a previous brand was known as Little Boy Blue whitener. In order to make sure that whites stayed white, bluing was put into the rinse water along with Clorox bleach. This was accomplished by stopping the cycle after the tub filled up for the rinse cycle and adding bluing. Hanging clothes out to dry in the sun further improved the product's bleaching qualities. Of course, depending upon one's socioeconomic status, spotlessness could be maintained without wetting one's hands. Some families employed household service workers while others farmed out their laundry to a local service worker who did laundry and ironing in her home. However, for those who wet their own hands, one washed not only personal items but also bed linens, curtains, napkins, tablecloths, and any other soiled or near-dirty item.

Tuesday was for ironing and mending. Any item of clothing that needed to be repaired waited until ironing day for its restoration. Before clothes could be ironed, those that were starched had to be wetted down and rolled up for an hour or two so that they would iron smoothly. This, of course, was before the popularity of the steam iron, which made that process unnecessary. Nothing escaped being ironed, even socks and underwear.

Clothes ironed on Tuesday were not put away until Wednesday. It was important to leave freshly ironed items hung up, laid out, or folded in the ironing room until the next day so that they would have a chance to "season," or set and fully dry, before being put away in the bureau where they would mildew if not completely dry.

Thursday was for many families either trash day or catch-all day, when one would catch up on whatever projects were left unfinished so they would not have to be carried over to their assigned day of the next week.

By Friday it was time for the house to have a full cleaning—not just a dusting, which was done daily—so that it could be ready for Sunday. This involved polishing the silver and doorknobs, scrubbing the woodwork around the door frames, and wiping down the walls.

Saturday was grocery day and cooking day. Preparing the Sunday dinner was a major event. All fresh ingredients had to be assembled and the meats selected for the dinner. Fresh fish, which was essential for so many southern Sunday breakfasts, had to be purchased from the local fishmonger or the local fisherman to make sure that it was absolutely fresh. And finally it was Sunday, the day of rest. Sunday was the day for attending church, eating with family and friends, and visiting relatives and community members who were sick or shut in.

The Norfolk of the 21st century reveals almost no remnants of this weekly routine. Today our lives are in the "to-go" mode, aided by computers, cell phones, and labor-saving appliances. Waiting time has been cut to a minimum for almost every activity, and household chores are squeezed in whenever possible, including Sundays. The old custom of sitting down at the table to have dinner as a family every evening has greatly diminished, if not disappeared altogether, in most homes. Daily meals of smothered chicken, pork chops, steak, or fried chicken, with macaroni and cheese, rice and gravy, mashed potatoes, or collard greens and dumplings that one anticipated going home to, are now little more than a fond memory or a pleasant tale told by a family elder.

Also long gone is the Sunday staple so necessary to sustain one through a long and intense church service, the classic Sunday breakfast. This morning feast began with fresh fruit, a sliced wedge of melon in the summer or orange sections or a half of grapefruit in winter, followed by fried fish—Norfolk spot or croaker—and grits, and each homemaker's pride, steaming hot rolls. The rolls were prepared on Saturday night when the dough was kneaded and put on the back of the stove to rise. Early Sunday morning, the dough was rolled out and shaped into rolls and set on a flat pan to rise for about two hours. While this was going on, the cook began to get partially dressed for church. Returning to the kitchen, the cook would begin to prepare breakfast after putting the rolls into the oven. She would fry the fish, cook the grits, and brew the coffee. There were many variations of the classic breakfast depending upon family tastes. But no matter how much it varied the main ingredient was always fish, either fried or baked, and hot rolls. A Sunday morning walk through most neighborhoods smelled like wandering through a bread factory. Sunday dinner after church was also a special time for the family and friends. This meal featured several choices of meats—fried chicken, ham or pork shoulder, and steak—and lots of side dishes of vegetables—corn, butter beans, snap peas, baked sweet potato, collard greens with dumplings, and stewed tomatoes. But the main event of Sunday's dinner was the desert. During the summer months, homemade ice cream was hand churned either early in the morning before breakfast, in which case the dasher or its remains were gathered and put into a special bowl to be saved for the young children. If the ice cream was made after church it was given to the young children to lick off the excess. This all went along with a peach cobbler or blueberry pie depending on what was in season. During the fall and winter the desert might consist of store-bought ice cream, but the pie—sweet potato or apple—would homemade.

To be fair, these meals would be far too time-consuming to prepare for the average modern household, especially those with both parents working outside the home. Family dinners have mostly been replaced by meals at fast food restaurants, primarily for the children. Or they have been replaced by meals at home with whoever is around when the meal, brought in or heated from frozen ingredients, is ready to eat. Long gone is the custom of dinner time as a chance for the family to gather and communicate after having been scattered throughout the day. Dinner time, which was usually between five and seven, used to be so sacrosanct that no one spoke on the phone then. Should anyone dare phone during dinner, they would be told that the person they were calling was having their dinner and would have to phone them back when they were finished.

Women today routinely work outside the home and even those who do not are usually engaged in childcare or volunteer activities, which consume large amounts of their time. An examination of the weekly routines of a modern family would reveal schedules that look more like those of corporate executives. Days are given to or built around interests and activities outside the home, sometimes extending to other cities entirely.

# 6. THE PEOPLING OF A MODERN CITY: 1910–2006

Norfolk had always been a welcoming harbor for people from other countries, particularly if they were from some part of Europe and could contribute to the local economy. Throughout the 18th and 19th centuries, Norfolk continued to welcome immigrants who were mainly from Europe: Scots, Irish, Russians (a generic name used for Poles and Lithuanians), and Germans. For the most part these groups were able to slot themselves into the economy without much fanfare. In most cases, having been merchants at home, many of them created similar jobs for themselves here. The German and Irish immigrants, however, often competed with and displaced the hired-out Africans for jobs as dock workers, service workers, and occasionally artisans. The pattern of immigration that established itself here was that those who came filled some sort of slot in the merchant class as shopkeepers, jobbers, street vendors, or the like. This was in sharp contrast to the immigration patterns at Ellis Island, where many of the newly arrived had only the shirt on their backs or the clothing in their bag. The Ellis Island pattern was probably the genesis of the classic American immigrant story, which is a variation on the Horatio Alger myth. The classic story, sometimes called the "fifty cents story" (probably because the immigrants are supposed to have had the absolute minimum amount of cash in their pockets), goes like this: The European peasants arrive in the United States with little or no resources other than what they could carry. Through hard work and a little luck, they become very wealthy within one generation. There were quite a few cases in which this did occur, but for the most part it took the average immigrants far longer to earn a livable wage, maintain their family, and acquire enough income to accumulate assets.

There is a Norfolk variation on this classic story. As people who came from immigrant backgrounds were interviewed for this project, the

Norfolk version was recounted time and again. Despite the occasional exception, Norfolk's immigration stories are far less harsh than the classic ones. Most people here explained that their families came to Norfolk to establish a better life of greater economic opportunity or to escape some form of oppression in their homeland. Most emphasized the devotion to hard work, the long grueling hours, and the personal sacrifice it took for them or their parents or grandparents to achieve an acceptable measure of material success. These stories, in addition to the emphasis placed on hard work, include recognition of the support and stability offered by the individual's ethnic community and the reassurance and guidance provided by their spiritual affiliation.

Reflecting on the immigrant experience in a recent *New York Times* article, Michael Slackman discussed the conundrum faced by third- and fourth-generation Circassians in Jordan: "The Circassian experience in Jordan is in many ways typical of the immigrant experience for many around the world. It is about holding on and letting go. Blending in and standing out." This has always been a dilemma for immigrants and their families. There is a large body of literature in academic journals on the subject of immigrant conflicts, especially with the second generation born in this country. While conflict between the arriving generation and the first and second generations existed in Norfolk also, the pressure was compounded by the fact that Norfolk was a racially segregated society in which only two races were recognized. Added to this was rampant, aggressive xenophobia. By most accounts, however, this conflict between those who originally immigrated and their Norfolk-born children was not as intense as it was in many other parts of the United States. The issues between parents and children could be worked through with the assistance of the immigrant groups' cultural organizing unit, which might be a secular or religious body. In some cases both were needed to set the terms of amelioration.

Even if the conflict of "holding on and letting go and blending in and standing out" was not as pronounced in Norfolk, it was not altogether unknown within Norfolk's immigrant community. In most cases, groups attempted to conceal these conflicts from outside eyes by presenting a harmonious and united facade. In his anniversary letter to the members of his congregation at the Greek Orthodox church, The Rev. Father Constantine Bithos alluded to frictions that have often arisen between those who came first—those who had to overcome many obstacles, the least of which was xenophobia—and those who arrived when the community was well established. Father Bithos reminded his parishioners:

> After those 50 years no one has or could have the same experience, because the people, who now come as immigrants have their relatives and friends, finding sympathy, work, education, and seldom have their smiles replaced by tears. . . . Not only are their intimate relatives waiting for them, but the American attitude has changed. It is much more sympathetic to the immigrants unlike the situation 50 years ago when the foreigner was an undesirable and was unscrupulously treated as a means rather than an end. . . . Some present day immigrants are rather unappreciative at the expense of their predecessors and relatives, who suffered and fought for the improvements of the advantages given to them by this blessed land of ours. Some say that "my uncle is illiterate; he is unschooled." The mere fact that his uncle or father does not know the art of writing and reading very well does not mean that he hasn't mastered the knowledge of his occupation and developed a wisdom that only experience and age can teach. . . . They swallowed their pride to make us proud. We are amazed today at their vision. This should not be called illiteracy, but courage and unselfishness.

The Greek community in Norfolk traces its beginnings back to the arrival of John Gretes in 1899. Two years later George Christopoulos and his wife Paraskevi arrived at the beginning of the new century. The record does not indicate what motivated these three to come to Norfolk; nevertheless, not long afterward the Greek community expanded to about 12. Since the church had been the center of their lives in Greece, the group banded together and began to worship in Old Saint Paul's Church. They rented the church for about $30 a month, an expense which they shared among themselves. The Rev. Father

Constantine Doropoulos of Baltimore came down to Norfolk to minister to their needs. This arrangement continued for approximately 10 years until the Norfolk congregation saved enough money to support a permanent priest. In order to do so, a request had to be made to the archbishop of Athens, Theoklitos. The request was granted and Archbishop Theoklitos appointed the Rev. Father George Smyrnakis. In addition, he sent the required liturgical items necessary for conducting mass. By the time of the first mass on March 3, 1911, there were 25 congregants. The mass was celebrated in the Old Christ and Saint Lukes Church, which was on Cumberland and Freemason Streets. The Old Christ Church was also rented for $30 a month.

The next step in the development of the Greek Orthodox Church in Norfolk was to establish a governing body. After writing a constitution and creating by-laws, a committee of George Christopoulos, George Karangelen, Archie Padis, Pericles J. Boogades, Constantine Kalevos, Chris Gabriell, Emanuel Constantinides, and James Constantopoulos served as members of a church governing body. By 1913, it was decided that a general assembly would be called in order to elect church officers and to select a board of trustees. The first person to serve as the president of the board was George Christopoulos, who was the oldest member of the community. He served two non-consecutive terms in 1913–1915 and 1918–1920. During Christopoulos's second term, Old Christ Church was purchased with the assistance of two other founding members, Pericles Boogades and Archie Padis. The structure on Granby Street was completed in 1955 and expanded several times to include an adjoining Sunday school wing, a classroom wing, and a community center wing to form the current church edifice.

Tom Vourlas was the first cantor for the Greek Orthodox Church, Annunciation. His son Nick Vourlas recounted his father's story in an interview, explaining that he immigrated in 1912 from Amphissa, 50 miles from Athens:

> When he first came here he lived in Indianapolis. I think he was there for about six years. The Greek church here was looking for a cantor and Harry Pappadis, who was the

president of the congregation, called my father and asked him to come to Norfolk to sing for the congregation. After about a year, Dad's mother wrote to him asking him to return to Greece to fight in the Greek army against the Turks and the Bulgarians. By 1914, he was back in Norfolk as the official church cantor.

The cantor essentially served as a one-man choir before church choirs were widespread. Vourlas sang during every Sunday service as well as on special occasions like funerals, weddings, and baptisms.

Vourlas returned to Norfolk after about three years and married, but his wife got sick and died in 1920:

About two years later, Dad married a woman he had known from his childhood who was newly arrived from Greece. Because she didn't speak any English, my little sisters and I spoke only Greek at home. I remember that we all lived in an apartment on top of the restaurant. I think this was the Dixie Restaurant. Dad had a total of three restaurants before he retired in 1955. The one which was my favorite was the diner in Berkley on South Main Street called the Virginia Lunch. Most of the customers were from the Coast Guard Station at the end of South Main Street and from the ship yard. In 1937 and '38 scrap metal was going to Japan daily. There were lots of workers and we had lots of business.

By the time I graduated from high school in 1940 I'd decided that I didn't want to be in the restaurant business. I wanted to go to school to study accounting. I had my sights on becoming an accountant. I don't know why but it appealed to me. These weren't my father's plans. Even though this was a disappointment to him, he allowed me to study at Norfolk Business College on Brooke Avenue and work part time in the restaurant. After graduating, I was able to get a job in the accounts payable department at Colonial Stores. Even though

I was young and inexperienced, I was assigned to work with a group of auditors who were doing a general audit. This was a very good experience for me at the time and I learned a lot.

When asked what made him feel Greek having lived in the United States all his life, Vourlas said it was his religion. "There are so many customs and rituals in the Orthodox Church that are also Greek customs that it is hard to think of being Greek without being Orthodox." An example, he said, is communion:

> In order to take communion, a person has to fast, not eating dairy products or meat on Wednesdays and Fridays, and there is no eating before church on Sunday. There are also certain foods associated with rituals or periods in our religion. These foods are Greek and I can't imagine being Greek without the foods, nor being Greek without being Orthodox. . . . Our church serves as the center of our community's spiritual and social life.

The role of the individual's spiritual community in maintaining and reinforcing the individual's sense of belonging and purpose cannot be overestimated. This is particularly evident in cases where spiritual affiliation, national identity, and culture are interwoven. This synthesis often produced a strong attachment to a spiritual connection in the form of a church, a synagogue, or a mosque.

Another group of immigrants whose identity revolved around their spiritual needs was Norfolk's Jewish community. According to Irwin Berent's *Norfolk, Virginia: A Jewish History*, the earliest known Jewish resident of this area was Jacob Abrahams, in 1786. Berent indicates that Abrahams was more than likely a shochet because his belongings contained, in addition to horses and furniture, a slaughterhouse. It seems reasonable that if Abrahams ran a slaughterhouse, there must have been enough Jewish residents in the area to support a business in kosher meats.

Moses Myers is regarded by most historians as being the first permanent Jewish resident of Norfolk. Myers was 34 when he arrived in 1887. His cousin Samuel, who accompanied him, was the son of a famous silversmith in New York. There is little information about what became of Samuel; however, Moses established an import-export business and became very financially successful. He is purported to have been one of Norfolk's first millionaires. It is known that he was not only a merchant, but was also very active in the civic life of Norfolk. As noted earlier, Myers was one of the non-Presbyterians who contributed funds for the establishment of the First Presbyterian church in Norfolk. This kind of ecumenicalism has characterized the Jewish community in Norfolk throughout its history in spite of periods of anti-Semitism. Members of Norfolk's Jewish community seem to have been able to surmount these difficulties through their commitment to full participation in the society and a willingness to share their resources with gentiles whenever needed and by their generous philanthropic efforts. The Jewish presence in Norfolk has been considerable not just for its size, but rather for the diversity and magnitude of its contributions to the civic, political, social, educational, and economic spheres.

Seldom mentioned in accounts of Norfolk's development are members of the Chinese American community. According to a 1995 *Virginian Pilot* column by George Tucker, Lee Sing was the first known Chinese to settle in Norfolk in 1885. Tucker does not reveal why Sing came to Norfolk; however, it is clear that he was here after the enactment of the Chinese Exclusion Law of 1882, which banned all Chinese workers from immigration to the United States. This suggests that Sing was already in the United States and moved to Norfolk from somewhere else in the country. Many of the Chinese workers who had originally settled in California to work in the gold mines and build the railroads increasingly found themselves no longer welcome around that time. But why Sing chose Virginia, and Norfolk specifically, is unknown. According to Tucker, Sing operated a laundry at 52 Bank Street. "By 1890, Sing had been joined by two compatriots, Lee Hing, whose laundry was at 226 Main Street and Wo Qoung, who operated at 18812 Church Street."

Tucker also recounted his experiences as a child in the early 1920s coming over from Berkley to Norfolk each Saturday to take music lessons. His route took him through the Chinatown section, which was at the time near the waterfront close to present-day Downtown Plaza. He described Chinatown as:

> A vastly different quarter from the rest of downtown. I saw mostly middle-aged or older men in black hats and loose-fitting clothing. Tantalizing odors emanated from the dark, small-windowed shops, where brightly packaged teas, straw-covered jars of preserved ginger and kumquats, dried fish, Chinese melons, exotic vegetables, and porcelains were displayed.

Tucker would not have known as a child the reason for the presence of so many males and the absence of females in the Chinese community. Since direct immigration from China was prohibited as of 1882, the immigration of Chinese women into most communities was greatly delayed. The only females available would have been from other parts of the United States. The first known female member of the Norfolk Chinese community was the grandmother of Yin Ma.

Norfolk's First Chinese Baptist Church traces its history to the prayer room in the Union Chinese Mission School. On May 5, 1901, an interracial and interdenominational group came together there to form the church." According to *A Brief History of the First Chinese Baptist Church,* "increased interest among this group of believers developed throughout the years, culminating in the formation of the formal and official organization of the First Chinese Baptist Church in 1928 and with the establishment of a church building at 306 East Freemason Street." Today the church is located in Virginia Beach on Pritchard Road and has a thriving, growing congregation with two pastors, one ministering to Chinese speakers and the other to the English speakers.

The Chinese American participation in Norfolk's development has been considerable. Until a few years ago, the corner of Virginia Beach Boulevard and Witchduck Road was known as "Chinese Corner." It is probable that the name came about because that corner was where Chinese day laborers gathered to be picked up for work as farmhands. The corner was also purported to have been the eastern boundary of a vast tract of Chinese-owned farmland from Military Highway in the west until the mid-20th century. Despite their contributions however, it is somewhat difficult to gather either written or anecdotal information on the Chinese community in Norfolk. Two of the main inhibitors are the language barrier that still exists and the reticence of some of the older members of the community and their reluctance to be interviewed.

The next large group to settle in Norfolk was from the Philippines. Filipino migration to the United States has been continuous since the early part of the 20th century. The relationship between the United States and the Philippines goes back to the end of the 19th century when the United States acquired the Philippines after the Spanish-American War of 1898. As citizens of a U.S. territory, Filipinos were regarded as American nationals and had the right to enter the United States without being subject to the Asian Exclusion Act of 1882.

According to oral histories compiled by the Filipino American National Historical Society, Hampton Roads Chapter, the U.S. Navy recruited in the Philippines from 1902 to 1992:

> Because of the Navy, a large concentration of Filipinos got their start in America in Hampton Roads. . . . Filipinos were the largest foreign ethnic group recruited by the United States government. Most Filipino men recruited from the Philippines entered the United States Navy as enlisted men relegated to work in mess halls, and serving as stewards to officers, admirals, and even presidents.

One of the longest surviving veterans in the Hampton Roads area was Marciano Malonzo, who served as a shop machinist for over 40 years. Both his affection for and his devotion to his job in the Navy was very typical of the way many Filipino Navy men felt towards their assignments here.

At the same time, Filipino women were also being recruited as nurses. Many young Filipinos in the Navy ended up marrying young Filipino nurses, and even sailors whose brides were not in the medical field could petition the government to allow their wives-to-be, as well as their families, to immigrate from the Philippines. The Navy provided housing for these new families, helping to ease their transition to life in the United States. Merrimack Park was one of the earliest and most frequently remembered Naval housing facilities available to Filipino families.

From 2003 through 2004 the Hampton Roads Chapter of the Filipino American National Historical Society mounted a project to collect the oral histories of Filipina women, affectionately known as "Aunties," who migrated to the Hampton Roads area as brides or sweethearts of enlisted Navy Filipino men. Many of the Aunties recounted publicly for the first time their experiences of being left alone as young brides with an infant or a few small children while their husbands were on deployment for six to seven months. The experience of Luz Igana recounted in *In Our Aunties' World: The Filipino Spirit of Hampton Roads*, is typical of the experiences of so many Navy wives from the Philippines: "You have to be strong if you want to be married to a military man. Every time your dad leaves, everything happens! . . . there's something wrong with the car or the plumbing is not working. . . . you think positive, you can do it. If there's a will there's a way. If you believe in God, that's the most important thing."

The largest influx of Filipinos to the Norfolk area coincided with the end of World War II and the beginning of the end of segregation. As with all immigrant groups, Filipinos were subject to the customs, attitudes, and laws of the time, a system of racial segregation and aggressive xenophobia. Much of their success in the face of these conditions was due in part to a world view they call *bahala na*, which loosely translates as, "come what may." This way of dealing with circumstances that come one's way in a positive manner, along with a sense of connectedness to community and a deep belief in Roman Catholicism, has sustained members of the Filipino community through many challenging situations here in Norfolk and in Hampton Roads. It has allowed Filipinos to survive, flourish, and prosper in their new home.

No discussion of immigrant contributions to Norfolk would be complete without a mention of the Lebanese community. Lebanese are known throughout the world for their business skills, and those who immigrated to Hampton Roads were no different. While their numbers are smaller here than on the peninsula, the area has been greatly enhanced by their participation. Attorney Pete Decker, or Uncle Pete as he is affectionately known, is Norfolk's ambassador of goodwill and the champion of all projects that benefit the city. And certainly, no visit to Norfolk would be complete without experiencing Doumar's on Montecello Avenue for ice cream in a handmade cone. Moreover, Norfolk's continuing face lift would not be as interesting and attractive had it not been for Barbara Zobys's contributions as chair of the city's Design Review Committee.

Although they are to a large degree invisible, there is another sizable group of contributors to the peopling of Norfolk and to its success. They are the thousands of migrants who came here from other regions of Virginia and the surrounding states of Maryland, North Carolina, West Virginia, Kentucky, and Tennessee to increase their opportunities for employment, schooling, and quality of life.

Finally, no mention of groups who have peopled the city would be complete without the inclusion of the men and women of the U.S. military who have come here from all over the country. There are so many who, after their length of service has finished, remain here to contribute their talents to the city and make Norfolk their home. There is a saying in the Navy that "once you have tasted Norfolk water, you stay."

# 7. The Challenges of a Modern City: 1910–2006

With the return of the troops along with new waves of immigrants, the period after World War II became a major turning point in Norfolk's history. As Forrest White explained in *Pride and Prejudice*:

> Two events alone make Norfolk's history at this time remarkable from that of other cities: one, the voracity of its assault upon urban blight; and two, the ferocity of its urban resistance to school desegregation. . . . Much that is both right and wrong with Norfolk today may be traced back to developments during the formative years between 1950 and 1960. . . . Before then, its citizens were far more attuned to the small town provincialism of rural Virginia than to the urban dynamism of the great port cities that were its competitors. . . . It was not until the close of World War II, when Norfolk stood on the brink of economic ruin, that its citizens found the courage to overthrow the political machine that had dominated its deliberations and stifled its advance.

This wave of change was signaled by the 1946 city council race between three competing forces: a new group calling themselves "The People's Ticket" comprised of wealthy professional and merchant interests, the old guard represented by the professional political incumbents, and a lone candidate, Victor I. Ash, who represented the African American community and other groups who were usually left out. Ashe's candidacy posed a real challenge to both sides. It threatened to upset the voting balance between the three incumbent candidates and the wealthy merchant challengers. Ashe, the first African American in modern times to run for a seat on the city council, encouraged his constituents, of which there were about 5,000 who were eligible to vote, to cast their vote for him alone. The reasoning was that this would deny the other candidates in the field their vote and almost assure Ashe's election, signaling a definitive shift in political power in the city.

The People's Ticket also represented change. The group was made up of major businessmen: Richard D. Cooke, a corporate attorney; Pretlow Darden, an automobile dealer; and John W. Twohy II, a wealthy concrete, sand, and gravel merchant. These men had not been involved in politics up until this race, instead focusing their considerable extracurricular energies on charitable volunteer projects. On the council side, the candidates were Mayor James W. Reed, Richard W. Ruffin, and C. Eddie Wright. As incumbents they represented business as usual and were closely aligned with the "Prieur Machine." William Prieur's position as clerk of courts belied both his influence and power. He was closely aligned with the state "Byrd Machine" and had exercised a great deal of control over city government since the Depression years. The city council under his influence had long represented stasis and a laissez-faire attitude toward rackets, prostitution, and moonshining. Moreover, the members of the city council were proponents of a policy of extreme fiscal conservatism, which was compounded by cuts in city services and, most importantly, a lack of interest in opening up Norfolk to outside development. To the regret of his African American supporters, the Victor Ashe strategy did not work. Nevertheless, the People's Ticket won and change did come to Norfolk's city government.

According to Parramore, Stewart, and Bogger in *Norfolk, The First Four Centuries*, the People's Ticket pledged to "cleanse Norfolk of its seedy image and reawaken the city's sense of pride and latent energies. They vowed that if elected they would serve only one term. . . . true to their campaign promises, they initiated a number of reforms which greatly facilitated the renaissance of sorts in Norfolk." There were 10 reforms credited with bringing Norfolk into the modern era: increases in property value assessment, retirement with pension plans for long term municipal workers, taking over control of the airport, establishing departments of safety and public works, increasing teachers' wages and school budgets, increasing enforcement of food-service laws, creating a Norfolk Portsmouth Tunnel and the Berkeley Bridge, initiating a study of street conditions to improving slums (approximately 20 percent of the city was occupied by slums and about 14 percent of the population lived in them and were responsible for more than 50 percent of the violent crime), reconfiguring the Norfolk Housing Authority, and finally, confirming that about 50 percent of the city's maintenance budget was spent on slums. In spite of the fact that the majority of the slum housing was non–owner occupied, the recommended solution was for redevelopment that would dislodge the tenants rather than go after the landlords. In hindsight, this particular initiative seems like more business as usual.

Nevertheless, with the new winds blowing through town, Norfolk came face to face with many of the issues that had haunted its history. Contributing to and in most cases hindering Norfolk's progress in becoming a major American port city on the size and scale of its competitors—New Orleans, New York, and Baltimore—were four recurring themes: a sense of impermanence, urban blight, lack of economic diversification, and ambivalence towards public education.

Even from its early days Norfolk engendered an underlying sense of impermanence fueled by a persistent series of calamities. This sense of temporariness began with the Virginia Company, as all settlers were in some way in their employ. The focus was on producing goods for export. When this effort proved to be insufficient and did not produce the volume and profits desired, the settlement became a colony and Norfolk's purpose and goals were imposed by the crown. The establishment of the city itself was for the purpose of creating a centralized collection point for goods from the outlying and surrounding areas. These goods, once received, were prepared for export to the West Indies and Europe. Norfolkians needed little reminder that all their efforts were for the benefit of England, and for a long time they were satisfied to see themselves in that way.

As the town grew, people became comfortable in their tasks and began to explore the idea of personal profit on the side—some for England and some for themselves. But as these notions of profit expanded, England tightened its restrictions, prohibiting trade with foreign nations and limiting it to crown colonies. The coup de grâce came in the form of taxation. As the colonists struggled to establish their rights, their city was burned to the ground during the Revolutionary War. This would not be the last time that Norfolk was demolished by fire. The early 19th century saw four major fires in a 30 year period. The first occurred in 1804 when 300 warehouses, stores, and dwellings were consumed by flames. The second came a year later when several houses on Water Street burned to the ground. In 1819, Bank Street tenements and other property on the north side of Main Street all the way to Talbot Street become casualties of the third major conflagration. The fourth major fire occurred in 1827 when Christ Church burned along with 60 neighborhood houses. Each time a part of the city was destroyed, it was rebuilt with substantial improvements. Nevertheless, the threat of destruction lingered.

Fire wasn't Norfolk's only destructive force—epidemics were also frequent. As an international port, Norfolk was vulnerable to whatever germs came along on arriving vessels. At least four times, in 1795, 1802, 1821, and 1826, Norfolk was host to the *Aedes aegypti* mosquito. Each outbreak left its mark on the city, causing loss of life and disruption to daily activities. Nevertheless, the town was ill prepared for the virulence of the Yellow Fever epidemic when it came in the summer of 1855. The outbreak raged for three long and grueling months, infecting everyone in its path. As fall arrived and the weather cooled, its intensity began to abate. By the time it finally subsided, 2,000 lives had been claimed.

Dr. George Armstrong, First Presbyterian's minister at the time, was the leading force in efforts to combat the disease. He and St. Patrick's Catholic pastor, Matthew O'Keefe, spent hours ministering to the sick and aiding in relief efforts. Dr. Armstrong later described his experiences in *A History of the Ravages of Yellow Fever in Norfolk, Virginia*. Even though Norfolk did not erect a monument to the thousands who lost their lives during this period, faithful citizens have decorated with plants and blooming flowers the headstone that sits on the northwest corner of Princess Anne Road and Hampton Boulevard, indicating the spot where many of the victims' bodies were interred in a mass grave.

The city's second recurring theme has been urban blight. The term implies a modern state of large-scale deterioration, but Norfolk's blight was an old condition deriving more from haphazard construction and structural overuse—assigning several families to live in structures designed for a single family—than from neglect. Almost from the beginning of the town, Norfolk's physical structure could best be described as shabby. As early as 1796, La Rochefoucauld commented in *Voyages dans les Etats-Unis* that Norfolk was "one of the ugliest, most irregular, dirtiest towns" he had ever seen. He was probably not exaggerating, since other visitors commented on the irregular, narrow, unpaved, dusty, poorly lit streets and the malodorous fumes emanating from the discarded rubbish and decomposing waste dumped into the Elizabeth River. Combined with all of that were the abundance of poorly constructed, and in some cases dilapidated, living structures.

The shabbiness was not because of a lack of interest in physical beauty, it derived more from lack of concern, or at least a neglect of concern for the overall look of the town itself. There is little evidence that in the early years of the 17th and 18th centuries much thought was put into the overall planning of the city beyond surveying the land and laying out the lots and streets. Any embellishment of the land was mostly left to the individual property owners. And foremost on most property owners' minds was the desire to establish a structure that would be suitable for conducting their business.

At the time of the creation of Norfolk's housing authority in 1940, slums cost Norfolk $750,000 a year in crime and disease. According to the authority, every time a proposal was made to eliminate the slum areas, "real estate interest balked, saying that slum clearance and public housing were not a legitimate function of government. It would have the effect of putting the government in competition with private interests." City Council agreed with them, even though two studies commissioned by the council strongly concluded that there was an urgent need for a housing agency to oversee slum clearance and the creation of suitable, affordable housing for working class citizens at the lower end of the economic scale. In 1940 the Navy issued a plea for "an authority to help build housing for national defense and military personnel," and the housing authority was finally created on July 30, 1940. One of the first public housing projects to be completed was Merrimack Park, constructed for Navy personnel. Construction was rapid and the first tenants were able to move in by April 1941.

According to the authority's 50th anniversary booklet, "In spite of a 69-percent expansion in housing during the Second World War—one of the largest in the nation—many of Norfolk's 10,000 returning veterans, many with brides, could only wish for homes of their own." The Housing Act of 1949, aided by the passage of Virginia legislation in 1946 to empower local authorities to "acquire, clear and make available to private enterprise, blighted areas for redevelopment" resulted in the creation of the Norfolk Housing and Redevelopment Authority, whose mission was expanded to include not only housing for military personnel and national defense but also redevelopment of the city's blighted areas. City Council was able to utilize this authority to begin redeveloping the city to ameliorate a whole list of ills that contributed to the city's stagnation.

The third theme that contributed to the stunting of Norfolk's growth was the lack of economic diversification. Looking over Norfolk's history it is hard to understand why in spite of repeated occurrences of suffering, hardships, and the penalties of encouraging a trade-only economy, Norfolk did not develop a significant alternate manufacturing base. If it had done so, it would not only have become a city that derived it revenue from being a service port for exports to the West Indies and Europe and an import harbor for southern and western Virginia and North Carolina, but also one which derived its revenue from producing a product that could meet a market demand in the national economy. To be fair, there were individual attempts of a sort in that direction, but those efforts were never a substantial contribution to the economy. Norfolk's industry developed largely to support its role in mercantile trade. One of the most dominant was shipbuilding, which remains to this day a major industry in Norfolk. All kinds of ancillary industries have sprung up that are necessary to support and supply the needed materials and products for this endeavor.

The fourth theme is ambivalence toward public education. In *Pride and Prejudice*, Forrest White notes that in the state of Virginia:

> Even in urban areas, secondary education was not universal, and was still the property of the middle class. Mandatory school attendance laws did not apply beyond the age of fourteen. . . .

the median education level for adults in Norfolk, with one of the finest school systems in the south, was still less than tenth grade, and more than one-fifth of the teenage population over fourteen had already dropped out of school. . . . It is against this backdrop of closed leadership, one man politics, and spotty support for public education that the concept of Massive Resistance faced its most important test in Norfolk.

Virginia's period of Massive Resistance, much like the Civil War period, can be viewed as one of the major moments in Norfolk history. Just as it had during the Civil War, this period marked a time when the city had to once again come to grips with the confluence of ideology, emotion, and pragmatism. For most of its history, Norfolk had the luxury of not having to involve itself with ideology. Decisions could be made based upon what was best for Norfolk, particularly what was in Norfolk's best economic interest. Usually what was best for Norfolk was what allowed its citizens to maintain the status quo. Norfolk has never been a city where intellectual considerations carried much cachet. Even during the Civil War, most people's support of the Confederacy had more to do with continuing business as usual and perpetuating a lifestyle rather than with grasping the benefits of industrialization for both the short and long haul.

Even though the much esteemed Virginian Thomas Jefferson proposed his Bill for the General Diffusion of Knowledge in 1779, education was never a major thrust for Virginians nor for Norfolkians in particular. In Jefferson's proposal, education was to be made available tuition free for three years to all male and female white children. Students would be taught the basic skills of reading, writing, and arithmetic and become familiar with Greek, Roman, English, and American history. Jefferson believed that by studying history, students would gain an understanding of human actions and sharpen their ability to reason and make moral choices. According to his plan this would provide the basic education for citizens in the new republic. In spite of Jefferson's proposal, education existed primarily for the children of the upper classes who were being groomed to take their place as heads of their families' assets or in the new leadership of the developing society.

Moreover, Norfolk was unlike many of the northern cities where there had been a large influx of non-Protestant European immigrants, primarily the Irish Catholic. There had been a long and continuing history of conflict between the English and the Irish that predated the colonial period. These antagonisms did not abate with the crossing of the water but rather continued to be fueled by differences in religious belief, particularly on the part of the English. The large immigration of Irish Catholics to northern industrial cities to work in the factories added to the desire to institute a public education system that would build nationalism, form a good citizen, protestantize Roman Catholics, and reform society. Horace Mann was the principal advocate for a "common" public school to which all children were assigned as the means of establishing social control with unified values and morals and cultural transmission in the form a common ideology, in this case the worship of the spirit of capitalism.

One of the chief reasons for a lack of interest in compulsory public schooling was that Norfolk's agrarian trade economy did not require masses of immigrants for its maintenance nor its success, which meant there were no masses of European peasants perceived to require socialization into the American way. For one thing, Norfolk had up until the Civil War a steady source of manageable workers who, because of enslavement, were plentiful, cheap, and always available. Even long after emancipation, a great number of African Americans occupied their former labor intensive slots within Norfolk society as agricultural farmhands, day labors, and service workers. Among the working class, both black and white, social status in Norfolk seemed to be derived less from one's occupation than from the amount of one's disposable income. In an odd sort of way the two did not seem to be connected in the way economics would suggest.

Norfolk's focus has always been on what was practical—practical for the making of money. And so the state's policy of Massive Resistance found Norfolk's citizens ready to comply more out of an emotional attachment to life as usual than out of a commitment to any ideological notion of equality of educational opportunity.

Massive Resistance was the name for the 1956 Virginia-initiated response to the U.S. Supreme Court's 1954 ruling in Brown v. Board of Education, integrating the nation's public schools. Virginia senator Harry F. Byrd pledged to fight the ruling by altering the administrative structure of the state public schools. Concurring with this position, the editor of the *Richmond News Leader* proposed in his defiant editorials that the state should interpose itself between the federal government and the public schools. As anachronistic as this notion might appear today, if for no other reason than that a war was waged and much blood spilled over the issue of whether the rights of the individual states had precedence over the rights of the nation as a whole, it was greeted with a great deal of support statewide. However, it should be pointed out that when Massive Resistance laws were enacted by the state legislature, Norfolk's school board was in the process of making plans to comply with the Supreme Court ruling. Two other Virginia cities, Warren County and Charlottesville, were also in the process of integrating by court order. Once the schools were ordered seized and closed by Gov. J. Lindsay Almond Jr., the Virginia General Assembly abolished the compulsory school attendance law, which had been one of the major requirements for the confederate states in the process of readmission to the Union.

Massive Resistance to public school integration also assigned the authority of school placement to newly created pupil placement boards, which were given the responsibility of awarding tuition grants to students who were opposed to school integration. The key to Massive Resistance was a law that withheld state funds from not only any school that complied with integration but also to any school that agreed to do so. Without state funding, public education could not survive no matter how determined the parents nor how dedicated the teachers. Once again Norfolk's response to the roadblock was to withdraw all white children from the schools slated for integration. Even though this was approximately 90 years later and both the climate and the context were different, Norfolk's citizens responded to forced integration as they had during the Civil War. This time the decision was imposed upon the city by the state, however.

Initially the majority of middle-income and affluent white Norfolk parents accepted the situation and began to arrange for their children to attend private church-organized schools, private tutoring academies, boarding schools, and various other private institutions. Less affluent parents, on the other hand, adopted a wait-and-see stance. They had neither the economic means nor the will to sustain private instruction for their children. Very few accounts of this period reveal the hardships and suffering imposed upon the poor, even though their number has been estimated at about 25 percent of the high school population.

On the other side, the majority of Norfolk's African American parents were not confronted with the same choices. First of all, there was only one non-white high school and it was not threatened with integration, so it remained open, as did all the African American junior highs. One peculiar aspect of the Massive Resistance laws was that they applied only to schools that were in the process of integrating. Since none of the "black" schools met that requirement, they were never closed and their students were never inconvenienced and continued to be educated daily. This odd set of circumstances was missed by most until finally the mayor and a city councilperson noticed. A proposal was put forward at council that resulted in a decision to rescind funding for all grades above sixth throughout the city. Surely, it was thought, this would punish the entire African American community for their resilience in withstanding Massive Resistance.

It was only the 17 students who had been selected to be test cases who had their education interrupted. The NAACP, so confident of their cause and so sure of their victory, decided that The Norfolk Seventeen, as these students were known, would not be returned to their regular schools but would instead wait out the appeal process. And so as the white churches had done, a school with its own principal, teachers, and administration was set up at First Baptist Church on Bute Street for the sole purpose of educating the Norfolk Seventeen. The curriculum paralleled the standard public school curriculum taught in the white high schools and junior highs. The teachers were regular Norfolk public school teachers, some retired and others still currently employed. All of them committed to aggressively educating the Norfolk Seventeen so that when integration came, as they felt confident it would, the students would not be behind their fellow classmates in their new integrated settings.

Throughout its history, Norfolk had wavered in its commitment to establishing strong, efficient public schools for its children. This time, the absurdity of denying secondary education to European American children, particularly those in the lower middle socioeconomic class, helped amplify the importance of an educated citizenry. No longer could Norfolk place education at the back of its list of priorities and maintain itself as a sleepy port of trade where education played second fiddle to turning a dollar. The Navy brought with it educated sailors and officers who required competent public education for their children. The Navy also brought abundant economic resources that were far too considerable for the city to ignore.

Change began in the 1990s, when the city government began an aggressive campaign to systematically address the four recurring themes that have plagued Norfolk's history and stymied its development. In the 1990s, the then school superintendent Dr. Gene R. Carter and the members of the school board, in conjunction with the city council, commissioned a special committee under the direction of Dr. Anna Dodson to research and design the model that would be used to attack the problem of poverty and ignorance. The committee's final report recommended the establishment of a comprehensive school program that would begin before kindergarten. The design for a comprehensive school setting included parents and their pre-school age children. The program itself would be housed in a school building using the entire space for activities devoted to pre-kindergarten learning and support services related to the enhancement of the children. The center would house a number of services designed specifically for their students such as social services, health services, comprehensive literacy, and exposure to music and art through activities such as circle time, small group time, and play. The idea was to provide experiences that would enable both the parents and their children to develop the skills, knowledge, and practical application necessary for success in their schooling and in life.

The first center was developed in the Berkley/Campostella area in 1991. This center, aptly called the Berkley/Campostella Early Childhood Education Center, is a comprehensive school setting. In addition to the traditional early childhood grouping of three- to five-year-olds—and true to its mission—the center accepts children from one month to three years old in a program called Even Start. Funding through Even Start has made it possible for parents to participate in this program. Working and non-working parents are encouraged to avail themselves of the training opportunities in the areas of home economics, job training, and high school equivalency courses that are offered through the program. Moreover, the faculty of the center are all state certified teachers with a specialization in early childhood education. Additionally all the assistant and classified workers are state certified "highly qualified" in accordance with the requirements of the No Child Left Behind Act.

According to the principal of the Berkley/Campostella Center, Cheryl Bunch, research has shown that "over the fifteen year period that we have been in existence, the longitudinal studies have indicated that our students out perform their peers in all areas. Norfolk has certainly been on the forefront of innovative educational initiatives to remedy at-risk conditions for its children." Since the inception of the first comprehensive early childhood center, two others have successfully replicated it in other parts of the city, one an early childhood center at Stuart and another at Oceanair Elementary School. Initiatives to remedy what Norfolk's school board sees as deficits to learning, development, and growth in producing fully participating citizens is ongoing. The success of Norfolk Public School initiatives in improving the quality of education was demonstrated in 2005 when it won the coveted Broad Prize. This prize is awarded annually to the urban school districts showing the greatest improvement in student achievement while also reducing performance gaps among ethnic groups and between income levels. Norfolk Public Schools had been a finalist for two previous years, in 2004 and 2003, before winning the top prize. Each recognition—as a two time finalist and as a winner—brought with it a cash prize. Norfolk received $125,000 each year as a finalist and $500,000 as the winner, for a total of $750,000. These funds are to be used to support four-year college scholarships for Norfolk public high school graduates.

Norfolk's Housing and Redevelopment Authority (NHRA) has not been idle either. In addition to its programs for lower income housing, it has been, in conjunction with the City Council, busy addressing the issue of urban blight by creating both a housing concept and a philosophy. Norfolk engaged the services of one of the leading gurus in "new urbanism," Ray Gindroz of Urban Design Associates, to consult in this effort. At a conference sponsored by NHRA and the Department of Planning and Community Development in 2003, Norfolk introduced *The Pattern Book for Norfolk Neighborhoods*, which signals "an important step in the overall refurbishment of many of our older and traditional neighborhoods that have both historical and architectural significance." The intent of the project was "to provide a resource for homeowners, builders and communities as they repair, rebuild and expand their houses and preserve their neighborhoods." Even though the ideas and designs in the book are preferred by the city, no attempt has been made to impose them through legislation. The city's thinking was that through education in the form of seminars and consultation at a centrally located street-level office, citizens could freely walk in to discuss their plans with a planner in the Neighborhood Design and Resource Center. This approach has gone a long way towards encouraging citizens to feel as though they are a part of the design of the city.

Realizing the need for mass transportation in the region, Norfolk also decided to institute a light rail system. Virginia Beach voted against the plan, citing its fears of uncontrolled access to the beach as one reason. To be fair, Virginia Beach has had difficulties maintaining order in the past when swarms of college-age youths invaded in search of sun and fun. This move is a clear indication that Norfolk's City Council recognizes the need for some form of mass transportation as a necessary ingredient in the development and maintenance of a modern urban city.

While Norfolk's efforts in the areas of impermanence and lack of economic diversity are somewhat less visible, it has certainly gone a long way towards conquering another old nemesis, fire. Norfolk has had for some time a very strong and up to date fire department that includes well trained firepersons who are cross-trained in fire prevention, management rescue, and emergency medical service. Programs in fire prevention, employee training, and response rates have greatly diminished the likelihood of total obliteration from a fire. Of course, structural improvements along with the institution of building codes rigorously enforced by well-trained inspectors and the establishment of a codes department to oversee and maintain enforcement have also helped. So that citizens can be an active part of the establishment and maintenance of building codes, Norfolk has what it refers to as the

Codes Academy. Citizens can take free courses in several subjects in order to learn about city codes. The Department of Community Development contains an active city planning department. To be in Norfolk today is like being in any other modern city that is being redeveloped and gentrified. On the other hand, very little if any of Norfolk's former character has been retained. In spite of a wonderful first class museum, an opera, a ballet, and a symphony, outside of its location, there is very little to distinguish Norfolk from "mid size city, USA."

The initiatives on economic diversity are also not as apparent as they are for some of the other themes. There is every reason to believe that the city council is aware of the lessons of history and that it has no desire to repeat those lessons. Nevertheless, Norfolk is still very much tied to the sea and to the U.S. Navy for its economic survival. Part of what inhibits Norfolk's economic diversification is its lack of buildable land. Norfolk, unlike its neighbor Chesapeake, does not have acres of open land available for the development of campus-style corporate offices. Nevertheless, even if Norfolk must forge a new and different path for itself, it appears to be well on its way. One could say that Norfolk is a city actively engaged in shoring up its deficits, charting its own course, and moving ahead in becoming a city to come home to now.